Bothersome *and disturbing* BIBLE PASSAGES

LOUIS R. TORRES

Printed by
Remnant Publications

Bothersome and Disturbing Bible Passages

This edition published 2013

Book Design: Tabatha D. Mattzela

Published by:
TorresLC Ministries
P.O. Box 688
Gaston, Oregon 97119

ISBN 10 0-9703553-5-1

ISBN 13 978-0-9703553-5-5

TABLE OF CONTENTS

Foreword

This book is written in response to the many inquiries that arise in the course of study at Mission College of Evangelism. Usually, those who make an effort to witness for Christ are confronted with texts that appear to say one thing when in reality they say something else. When these verses of Scripture are brought before them, they find themselves unable to respond. Though the text seems to contradict what they sense the Bible says, at that moment they find themselves lost for words.

It is hoped that this little book will give greater confidence to those who are desirous of sharing the "faith that is within them," and that this confidence will lead them to the conviction that they have not followed "cunningly devised fables," but rather the truth as it is in Christ.

It is also the purpose of this work to assist those who become confused when coming across these verses of Scripture. I have been a victim of these kinds of confrontations, whether from an opponent of my particular beliefs, or just finding myself troubled by mysterious passages that appear to controvert the very foundation of my faith. I have had to struggle with seemingly contradictory texts, but through much study and prayer have received the help of the Lord to finally see the light in the perfect harmony of God's word.

There is a strong conclusion that has surfaced over and over again in my studies: God does not contradict Himself. Therefore, it is irresponsible for a person to take one text and in exclusion to the rest of the scriptures make a doctrine. The prophet Isaiah says, "For precept must be upon precept, precept upon precept; line upon line, line upon line; here a little, and there a little" (Isaiah 28:10).

May this little book serve to take those rough, turbulent moments and smooth the tide of controversy into a quiet, peaceful haven of truth.

Author

OLD TESTAMENT

Genesis 2:25
And they were both naked, the man and his wife,
and were not ashamed.

Answer

There are those who assume that Adam and Eve were walking in the nude in the Garden of Eden. However, the language of verse 25 follows 23 and 24, which is speaking about the first marriage and God's declaration that the "man and his wife" can be naked in the presence of each other and not be ashamed. After all, they become one flesh! That wandering naked around the garden was not acceptable is evident. When Adam and Eve sinned and saw that they were naked, they "sewed fig leaves together, and made themselves aprons" (Genesis 3:7). This scanty covering was not acceptable to God, so He made them "coats of skins, and clothed them" (verse 21). Adam and Eve must have been covered with the same robe of righteousness that the righteous will be clothed with in the new earth. John saw "a great multitude, which no man could number, of all nations, and kindreds, and people, and tongues, stood before the throne, and before the Lamb, clothed with white robes, and palms in their hands" (Revelation 7:9). When Adam and Eve sinned, they lost their covering, which rendered them naked.

Jesus said, "He that overcometh, the same shall be clothed in white raiment; and I will not blot out his name out of the book of life, but I will confess his name before my Father, and before his angels." "I counsel thee to buy of me gold tried in the fire, that thou mayest be rich; and white raiment, that thou mayest be clothed, and that the shame of thy nakedness do not appear; and anoint thine eyes with eyesalve, that thou mayest see" (Revelation 3:5, 18). God's people will ever be clothed in the pristine eternal beauty of the new earth. Once more they will walk in innocence. But notice that they are not restored to nakedness; rather, they are clothed with glory.

Genesis 4:17

And Cain knew his wife; and she conceived, and bare Enoch: and he builded a city, and called the name of the city, after the name of his son, Enoch.

Answer

Questions have been raised concerning the wife of Cain. There is an assumption that there were other people on the earth and, therefore, Adam and Eve were not the only beings created. The Scriptures only record the creation of two persons. "God created man in his own image, in the image of God created he him; male and female created he them" (Genesis 1:27). First He created man (Genesis 2:7). Then, since man was the only being (Genesis 2:18), He took a bone out of man's side and made a woman" (Genesis 2:21-23). Eve is called the "mother of all living" (Genesis 3:20). Consequently, there could not have been any other people apart from her. Cain got his wife from one of his relatives. The reason for this conclusion is that Adam and Eve had "sons and daughters." (See Genesis 5:4.) God had commanded Adam and Eve to "be fruitful, and multiply, and replenish the earth" (Genesis 1:28). This could only be done as brother and sister fulfilled that command. Men were giants (Genesis 6:4) and had just recently come from the Creator's hand. Because of this, they were capable of marrying family members without the modern-day complication.

Then came the Flood. After the Flood there were only four couples that survived (Genesis 7:22, 23). In order to repopulate the earth, intermarriage had to be practiced again. According to Jesus' own words, He said, "Have ye not read, that he which made them at the beginning made them male and female, And said, For this cause shall a man leave father and mother, and shall cleave to his wife: and they twain shall be one flesh? Wherefore they are no more twain, but one flesh. What therefore God hath joined together, let not man put asunder" (Matthew 19:4-6). From these words spoken in Eden concerning Adam and Eve (Genesis 2:24), we conclude that the Creator Himself confirms only two original created beings.

Genesis 6:2, 4

That the sons of God saw the daughters of men that they were fair; and they took them wives of all which they chose. There were giants in the earth in those days; and also after that, when the sons of God came in unto the daughters of men, and they bare children to them, the same became mighty men which were of old, men of renown.

Answer

There are some whose interpretation considers these verses as referring to angels that came down from heaven and married women. It is true that the phrase "sons of God" is used in the Bible when speaking about celestial beings. The references are found three times in the book of Job (Job 1:6; 2:1; and 38:7). Apparently, representatives from God's universe gathered together for a special meeting, and Satan interjected himself as the rightful representative of planet Earth (Job 1:6, 7). Nevertheless, this title is not solely used for celestial beings.

This same expression is utilized in the rest of the Bible when speaking about the faithful children of God on the earth. The texts are John 1:12; Romans 8:14, 19; Philippians 2:15; and 1 John 3:1, 2. After the fall of man there developed two groups of people that began to multiply on the earth. Those from the line of Seth (See Genesis 5:6-32) are considered to be the progenitors of the righteous, and those from the line of Cain are considered to be the unrighteous or wicked. (See Genesis 4:15-24.) Jesus, in referring to the two classes of people, said, "The good seed are the children of the kingdom; but the tares are the children of the wicked one; The enemy that sowed them is the devil" (Matthew 13:38, 39).

In the book of Matthew, Christ made reference to this period of time, saying, "For as in the days that were before the flood they were eating and drinking, marrying and giving in marriage, until the day that Noe entered into the ark, And knew not until the flood came, and took them all away; so shall also the coming of the Son of man be" (Matthew 24:38, 39). Note that Jesus does not mention angels but rather the antediluvians (the ill-prepared humans) that were marrying and giving in marriage. Christ very clearly states concerning angels, "For in the resurrection they neither marry, nor are given in marriage, but are as the angels of God in heaven" (Matthew 22:30). Angels do not marry! In the book of Luke the words of Jesus further clarify this point and distinguishes the two classes. "And Jesus answering said unto them, The children of this world marry, and are given in marriage: But they which shall be accounted worthy to obtain that world, and the resurrection from the dead, neither marry, nor are given in marriage: Neither can they die any more: for they are equal unto the angels; and are the children of God, being the children of the resurrection" (Luke 20:34, 35). This may be a thought to ponder, but man is the only one capable of reproduction.

From what Jesus said, angels were not given that prerogative.

At some point before the Flood these two classes of people began to merge. Hence "the sons of God," or the righteous, intermarried with the "daughters of men," or the wicked ones. The amalgamation contributed to diluting the spiritual condition of the righteous. This brought about the situation on the earth that left only a few "sons of God" such as Methuselah, Enoch, and finally Noah and his family (eight in number). In the Flood the righteous were spared, but the rest were destroyed. The apostle Peter writes, "And spared not the old world, but saved Noah the eighth person, a preacher of righteousness, bringing in the flood upon the world of the ungodly."

It is this unholy union that brought the defeat to the Israelites (Numbers 31:15, 16) and Samson (Judges 14:1-3), and that no doubt prompted the apostle Paul to issue the following admonition: "Be ye not unequally yoked together with unbelievers: for what fellowship hath righteousness with unrighteousness? and what communion hath light with darkness? And what concord hath Christ with Belial? or what part hath he that believeth with an infidel?" (2 Corinthians 6:14, 15).

Genesis 9:3
Every moving thing that liveth shall be meat for you; even as the green herb have I given you all things.

Answer
The original diet in Genesis 1:29 consisted of nuts, fruits, and grains. The animals' food was the "green herb" (Genesis 1:30). After the fall of man, God added the "herb of the field" to his diet (Genesis 3:18). Before the Flood, God instructed Noah and said, "And take thou unto thee of all food that is eaten, and thou shalt gather it to thee; and it shall be for food

for thee, and for them" (Genesis 6:21). Notice that prior to the Flood, God made it clear to take "all food that is eaten." This command suggests that there was a knowledge concerning what was food. And also that at this time of earth's history flesh was not included as being part of this definition. Not all that God had made was for food. This food thus stored in the ark was to serve them and the animals as provision during and after the Flood until the edible vegetables grew back again.

Then, at some point after the Flood, God allowed the use of flesh food for the first time. The clean animals were more in number (in seven pairs), and the unclean by two in number (Genesis 7:2). The Lord allowed them to use flesh for food from among the clean. It was only from the clean animals also that sacrifices were offered (Genesis 8:20). The unclean animals never consisted as part of either the sacrificial services or the diet of God's people. Had the unclean been used for food they would have become extinct, since there was only one pair of each in the ark.

However, there were consequences that came along with the permission of flesh eating. "But flesh with the life thereof, which is the blood thereof, shall ye not eat. And surely your blood of your lives will I require; at the hand of every beast will I require it, and at the hand of man; at the hand of every man's brother will I require the life of man" (Genesis 9:3-5). After the Flood, man's lifespan was reduced from nine hundred-plus years (Genesis 5:5, 8, 11, 14, 20, 27) to around one hundred-plus years (Genesis 25:7; 35:28). In the same way that not all plant life was to be eaten, so not all flesh was to be eaten. The term "every moving thing" must be taken in the same manner as "even as the green herbs." That is to say, not everything is for food.

Genesis 35:18

And it came to pass, as her soul was in departing, (for she died) that she called his name Benoni: but his father called him Benjamin.

Answer

This text has posed a challenge to many. It appears to say that her soul was leaving her as she was dying. The explanation is found in the way that God in the writings of Moses uses the word "soul." In chapter 2 the first appearance of the word "soul" is found. "And the LORD God formed man of the dust of the ground, and breathed into his nostrils the breath of life; and man became a living soul" (Genesis 2:7). A "living soul" is the composite of two elements — body plus breath. This combination equals a "live being" or a "person." This concept is continued in the writings of Moses. Notice the following texts: "Say, I pray thee, thou art my sister: that it may be well with me for thy sake; and my soul shall live because of thee." "And the uncircumcised man child whose flesh of his foreskin is not circumcised, that soul shall be cut off from his people; he hath broken my covenant." "Behold now, this city is near to flee unto, and it is a little one: Oh, let me escape thither, (is it not a little one?) and my soul shall live" (Genesis 12:13; 17:14; 19:20). Notice that both Abraham and Lot expressed concern for their soul, or in other words, were worried about the loss of their lives.

With this perspective, the phrase "as her soul was in departing" simply meant "while at the brink of death" she gave birth and died. Verse 19 says, "And Rachel died, and was buried in the way to Ephrath, which is Bethlehem." Later on in the book of Numbers. Moses wrote, "And the priest shall make an atonement for the soul that sinneth ignorantly, when he sinneth by ignorance before the LORD, to make an atonement for him; and it shall be forgiven him" (Numbers 15:28). Like Moses, Ezekiel employed the same usage of synonyms when he wrote: "The soul that sinneth, it shall die. The son shall not bear the iniquity of the father, neither shall the father bear the iniquity of the son: the righteousness of the righteous shall be upon him, and the wickedness of the wicked shall be upon him" (Ezekiel 18:20).

Exodus 4:21

And the LORD said unto Moses, When thou goest to return into Egypt, see that thou do all those wonders before Pharaoh, which I have put in thine hand: but I will harden his heart, that he shall not let the people go.

Answer

Perhaps this verse more than any other has been employed to show that people are "set up" by God for His own egotistical purpose. The truth of the matter is that Pharaoh hardened his own heart.

In the other chapters of Exodus we read: "But when Pharaoh saw that there was respite, he hardened his heart, and hearkened not unto them; as the LORD had said. And Pharaoh hardened his heart at this time also, neither would he let the people go." "And when Pharaoh saw that the rain and the hail and the thunders were ceased, he sinned yet more, and hardened his heart, he and his servants" (Exodus 8:15, 32; 9:34). Even the Philistines during the days of Eli the high priest recognized that Pharaoh hardened his own heart. "Wherefore then do ye harden your hearts, as the Egyptians and Pharaoh hardened their hearts? when he had wrought wonderfully among them, did they not let the people go, and they departed?" (1 Samuel 6:6).

Why does it say that God hardened his heart? Because God is the one who brought the test to Pharaoh. This language is the same as that of a person saying, "If he hadn't hit me, I would not have hit him," or, "He made me do it," implying that the reaction came in direct response to the action. Or perhaps you have said, "I made him angry by what I have said." The reality is that a person makes himself angry depending on his response to the issue. This concept is seen in the attitude of King Zedekiah.

"Zedekiah was one and twenty years old when he began to reign, and reigned eleven years in Jerusalem. And he did that which was evil in the sight of the LORD his God, and humbled not himself before Jeremiah the prophet speaking from the mouth of the LORD. And he also rebelled against king Nebuchadnezzar, who had made him swear by God: but he stiffened his neck, and hardened his heart from turning unto the LORD God of Israel" (2 Chronicles 36:11-13).

The people on the day of Pentecost felt an unseen influence. It says, "They were pricked in their hearts" (Acts 2:36). God was the "protagonist," the Jews were the object of the action. They now had to respond to the divine influence. Fortunately, they responded positively. "Now when they heard this, they were pricked in their heart, and said unto Peter and to the rest of the apostles, Men and brethren, what shall we do?" (Acts 2:37). Had they not responded positively, the pricking would have resulted in their "hardening their hearts." Hence, in this sense, God would have hardened their heart.

Exodus 16:29

See, for that the LORD hath given you the sabbath, therefore he giveth you on the sixth day the bread of two days; abide ye every man in his place, let no man go out of his place on the seventh day.

Answer

This command was given to the Jews in reference to the gathering of manna. In verse 25 there is further clarification: "Today is the Sabbath unto the Lord: today ye shall not find it in the field." In other words, provision had already been made for their food on the day before. (See verse 26.) Some use this text to forbid any travel on the Sabbath. However, Jesus traveled to Nazareth and "went into the synagogue on the Sabbath day" (Luke 4:16). The apostles likewise traveled on the Sabbath. "And on the Sabbath day we went out of the city by a river side, where prayer was wont to be made" (Acts 16:13). Proper travel is appropriate on the Sabbath.

Exodus 20:4

Thou shalt not make unto thee any graven image, or any likeness of any thing that is in heaven above, or that is in the earth beneath, or that is in the water under the earth.

Answer

There are those who conscientiously consider this commandment as forbidding the making of any religious illustration, photography, or the fine arts. Deuteronomy chapter 4 is also cited in this prohibition: "And he declared unto you his covenant, which he commanded you to perform, even ten commandments; and he wrote them upon two tables of stone. And the LORD commanded me at that time to teach you statutes and judgments, that ye might do them in the land whither ye go over to possess it. Take ye therefore good heed unto yourselves; for ye saw no manner of similitude on the day that the LORD spake unto you in Horeb out of the midst of the fire: Lest ye corrupt yourselves, and make you a graven image, the similitude of any figure, the likeness of male or female, The likeness of any beast that is on the earth, the likeness of any winged fowl that flieth in the air, The likeness of any thing that creepeth on the ground, the likeness of any fish that is in the waters beneath the earth: And lest thou lift up thine eyes unto heaven, and when thou seest the sun, and the moon, and the stars, even all the host of heaven, shouldest be driven to worship them, and serve them, which the LORD thy God hath divided unto all nations under the whole heaven" (Deuteronomy 4:13-19). This commandment is all-inclusive. It forbids attempting to make an image of God, who they did not see; it also prohibits making a likeness of an animal, man, fowl, insect, or fish. The word "likeness" means a pattern, or similitude of any of these things. The question is, What is God forbidding? Is He forbidding the making of graven images, or the worshiping of them?

If God is solely prohibiting the making of graven images then He violated His own counsel. For it was He that instructed Moses to make and place cherubims in the tabernacle (Exodus 25:18-22), and angels inwrought on the curtains (Exodus 26:1). Oxen, lions, and angels were made in Solomon's temple (1 King 6:23-35; 7:29, 36). In the desert God instructed Moses to make a brazen serpent representing Christ (Numbers 21:8, 9; John 3:14). However, when they began to venerate it, it was destroyed (2 Kings 18:4). Obviously, if the making of images violates the commandment, then all pictures, statuaries, paintings, and any likeness of anything animate or inanimate should be destroyed. But since it is not the case that God is prohibiting the making of statuaries, then what is the second commandment forbidding?

In both references relating to the second commandment we find the words: "Thou shalt not bow down thyself to them, nor serve them" and "be driven to worship them" (Exodus 20:5; Deuteronomy 4:19). The main focus is making images and worshiping or venerating them. Though the angels were known by the Israelites to be inside the tabernacle, they were not allowed to worship them. The people were to worship God alone, never the angels (Revelation 19:10; Isaiah 6:10). God's concern was clearly with the temptation to use images as worship aids. The Lord is telling the Hebrews, "Don't you in any way make worship of Me dependent on artistic worship aids. Worship me directly, from the heart." God is a lover of beauty; the tabernacle and Solomon's temple are perfect examples of this. He is the one who endowed Bezaleel and Aholiab with the skills to make the fine work of art that went into making the tabernacle and its imagery (Exodus 36). Art was made for beauty, never as objects of worship.

Exodus 20:5, 6

For I the LORD thy God am a jealous God, visiting the iniquity of the fathers upon the children unto the third and fourth generation of them that hate me; and shewing mercy unto thousands of them that love me, and keep my commandments.

Answer

Some have mistaken this part of the second commandment assuming that God punishes the posterity of parents for the sins they have committed. But this is not the case. The same writer that recorded this commandment states, "The fathers shall not be put to death for the children, neither shall the children be put to death for the fathers: every man shall be put to death for his own sin" (Deuteronomy 24:16). The prophet Ezekiel wrote, "When the son hath done that which is lawful and right, and hath kept all my statutes, and hath done them, he shall surely live. The soul that sinneth, it shall die. The son shall not bear the iniquity of the father, neither shall the father bear the iniquity of the son: the righteousness of the righteous shall be upon him, and the wickedness of the wicked shall be upon him" (Ezekiel 18:19, 20). In fact verses 1-18 address this issue.

The commandment is simply stating that those that follow the sinful practices of their parents, unto the third and fourth generations, and hate God will suffer the consequences. Likewise, those who love and keep the commandments of the Lord will reap from His mercies.

Exodus 34:28

And he was there with the LORD forty days and forty nights; he did neither eat bread, nor drink water. And he wrote upon the tables the words of the covenant, the ten commandments.

Answer

It appears from this text that Moses wrote the Ten Commandments. The problem is simply in the grammatical structure. The context is clear. In the first verse the Lord said, "Hew thee two tables of stone like unto the first." Moses is with the Lord and "he," the Lord, writes the commandments. Deuteronomy states the same fact. "At that time the LORD said unto me, Hew thee two tables of stone like unto the first, and come up unto me into the mount, and make thee an ark of wood. And I will write on the tables the words that were in the first tables which thou brakest, and thou shalt put them in the ark. And I made an ark of shittim wood, and hewed two tables of stone like unto the first, and went up into the mount, having the two tables in mine hand. And he wrote on the tables, according to the first writing, the ten commandments, which the LORD spake unto you in the mount out of the midst of the fire in the day of the assembly: and the LORD gave them unto me" (Deuteronomy 10:1-4). At no time did God allow Moses to be the inscriber of His holy law. God wrote it with His own finger (Exodus 31:18; Exodus 34:1; Deuteronomy 9:10).

Leviticus 3:17
It shall be a perpetual statute for your generations
throughout all your dwellings,
that ye eat neither fat nor blood.

Answer
I have met some people from a particular denomination that use this text as a proof text against blood transfusion. First of all, blood transfusion is not the issue, since that practice never existed in those days. It was the eating of the blood of animals that was the issue. Hundreds of years before God gave this admonition to the Jews, He said to Noah and his family, "But flesh with the life thereof, which is the blood thereof, shall ye not eat" (Genesis 9:4). This same prohibition the Lord made in the New Testament: "That ye abstain from meats offered to idols, and from blood, and from things strangled, and from fornication: from which if ye keep yourselves, ye shall do well. Fare ye well" (Acts 15:29). In transfusion, it is human blood that is used, not that of animals. Jesus' question to the Jews is applicable when it comes to saving life. "Then said Jesus unto them, I will ask you one thing; Is it lawful on the sabbath days to do good, or to do evil? to save life, or to

destroy it?" (Luke 6:9). In other words, if it was important to save life even on the Sabbath, then it important to save lives at other times. Transfusions have saved thousands of lives.

Numbers 15:32, 35

And while the children of Israel were in the wilderness, they found a man that gathered sticks upon the Sabbath day. And the LORD said unto Moses, The man shall be surely put to death: all the congregation shall stone him with stones without the camp.

Answer

The argument is made that since stoning of Sabbath breakers is not enforced any longer, then it is not wrong to break or disregard the Sabbath. The truth is that under the theocracy several flagrant transgressions were meted out the same punishment. Stoning for adultery (Leviticus 20:10), for blasphemy (Leviticus 24:16), an ox that gored a man (Exodus 21:28), for stealing (Joshua 7:25), and of mediums or psychics (Leviticus 20:27) was the punishment. Even in Christ's day, adultery was still punished by stoning (John 8:4, 5). Though today we are no longer living under God's direct rule, does it make these acts right? All of these transgressions are still considered wrong, but stoning is not the punishment meted out. Will these sins be punished? Yes! God says, "Know ye not that the unrighteous shall not inherit the kingdom of God? Be not deceived: neither fornicators, nor idolaters, nor adulterers, nor effeminate, nor abusers of themselves with mankind, Nor thieves, nor covetous, nor drunkards, nor revilers, nor extortioners, shall inherit the kingdom of God" (1 Corinthians 6:9, 10). Just as no one in their right mind would consider these offenses permissible, neither should license be sought for disregarding the fourth commandment.

Deuteronomy 4:13

And he declared unto you his covenant, which he commanded
you to perform, even ten commandments;
and he wrote them upon two tables of stone.

Answer

In theological terms a covenant is an agreement that brings
about a relationship of commitment between God and
His people. God made several covenants with His people.
He made one with Noah (Genesis 9:9-17), with Abraham
(Genesis 15:18), Moses, and with David (2 Samuel 23:1-5). The
dispensationalist's doctrine mistakenly takes this reference of
the Ten Commandments and applies it to the old covenant
that was done away with. Though the commandments were
part of the covenant, they did not pass away. The Bible
declares the commandments to be "perfect" (Psalm 19:7),
but the old covenant had "fault" (Hebrews 8:7, 8). The old
covenant mentioned is not the Ten Commandments. Jesus
declared, "For verily I say unto you, Till heaven and earth
pass, one jot or one tittle shall in no wise pass from the law, till
all be fulfilled." Obviously, heaven and earth have not passed!

Concerning the old covenant, Paul says, "In that he saith, A
new covenant, he hath made the first old. Now that which
decayeth and waxeth old is ready to vanish away" (Hebrews
8:13). The vanishing away of the covenant had already taken
place in Paul's day. But the passing of heaven and earth is
yet future. Concerning the law, God says, "Let us hear the
conclusion of the whole matter: Fear God, and keep his
commandments: for this is the whole duty of man. For God
shall bring every work into judgment, with every secret
thing, whether it be good, or whether it be evil" (Ecclesiastes
12:13, 14)." "For whosoever shall keep the whole law, and

yet offend in one point, he is guilty of all. For he that said, Do not commit adultery, said also, Do not kill. Now if thou commit no adultery, yet if thou kill, thou art become a transgressor of the law. So speak ye, and so do, as they that shall be judged by the law of liberty" (James 2:10-12). It is the everlasting law of liberty that God will use as a standard for the judgment. The judgment is also in the future. If He indeed did away with His standard, then there could be no judgment.

Deuteronomy 5:2-4

The LORD our God made a covenant with us in Horeb. The LORD made not this covenant with our fathers, but with us, even us, who are all of us here alive this day.
The LORD talked with you face to face
in the mount out of the midst of the fire.

Answer

The covenant referred to has its foundation in the Ten Commandments. Because of these verses, some interpret them as meaning that the law was not applied to anyone before the commandments were written on Sinai. But this conclusion is not correct. In a careful analysis of the temptation of Eve one can quickly see that she was tempted to be another god, breaking the first commandment — committing selfmurder (the sixth commandment), taking that which did not belong to her (the eighth commandment), desiring the fruit to make one wise (the tenth commandment), and not honoring her father (the fifth commandment). (See Genesis 3:1-6). Concerning Abraham it says, "Because that Abraham obeyed my voice, and kept my charge, my commandments, my statutes, and my laws" (Genesis 26:5). Joseph knew that adultery was a sin (Genesis 39:7-9). Until the law was written, the oracles of God had been passed on by word of mouth from generation to generation.

The words of Moses have to do with the agreement that God was specifically making with Israel as a nation. It was not the patriarchs who stood before God at Sinai; it was the Israelites whom God addressed and spoke to. They were the ones alive at that time, and they, not their forefathers, had to take responsibilities for their part of the agreement. Moses reminded them later that the covenant had also been made with their forefathers. "That thou shouldest enter into covenant with the LORD thy God, and into his oath, which the LORD thy God maketh with thee this day: That he may establish thee to day for a people unto himself, and that he may be unto thee a God, as he hath said unto thee, and as he hath sworn unto thy fathers, to Abraham, to Isaac, and to Jacob" (Deuteronomy 29:12-13). Many years later, King David reminded them of this fact. He wrote, "Be ye mindful always of his covenant; the word which he commanded to a thousand generations; Even of the covenant which he made with Abraham, and of his oath unto Isaac; And hath confirmed the same to Jacob for a law, and to Israel for an everlasting covenant" (1 Chronicles 16:15-17).

Deuteronomy 5:14, 15

But the seventh day is the sabbath of the LORD thy God: in it thou shalt not do any work, thou, nor thy son, nor thy daughter, nor thy manservant, nor thy maidservant, nor thine ox, nor thine ass, nor any of thy cattle, nor thy stranger that is within thy gates; that thy manservant and thy maidservant may rest as well as thou. And remember that thou wast a servant in the land of Egypt, and that the LORD thy God brought thee out thence through a mighty hand and by a stretched out arm: therefore the LORD thy God commanded thee to keep the sabbath day.

Answer

The explanation to this text has to do with remembering "that thou wast a servant in the land of Egypt." Moses is not saying that the Sabbath is a memorial of the exodus from Egypt. For it was he who wrote, "And on the seventh day God ended his work which he had made; and he rested on the seventh day from all his work which he had made. And God blessed the seventh day, and sanctified it: because that in it he had rested from all his work which God created and made" (Genesis 2:2,3). He also recorded the fourth commandment in the scriptures that said: "Remember the sabbath day, to keep it holy. Six days shalt thou labour, and do all thy work: But the seventh day is the sabbath of the LORD thy God: in it thou shalt not do any work, thou, nor thy son, nor thy daughter, thy manservant, nor thy maidservant, nor thy cattle, nor thy stranger that is within thy gates: For in six days the LORD made heaven and earth, the sea, and all that in them is, and rested the seventh day: wherefore the LORD blessed the sabbath day, and hallowed it" (Exodus 20:8-11). In these verses He makes it obvious that the Sabbath is a memorial of creation and the Creator.

In these verses Moses is addressing the need to use recollection of their lot in Egypt as a means of not treating their servants as they were treated. It is the same as saying, "In the Egyptian bondage they tried to work you to death without rest, but God brought you out and gave you rest." Therefore, "if a stranger sojourn with thee in your land, ye shall not vex him … for ye were strangers in the land of Egypt" (Leviticus 19:33, 34). In regard to a Hebrew being sold as a bondman, God instructed that they treat them fairly, reminding them that, "thou shalt remember that thou wast a bondman in the land of Egypt, and the LORD thy God redeemed thee: therefore I command thee this thing today" (Deuteronomy 15:15).

Deuteronomy 14:21

Ye shall not eat of any thing that dieth of itself: thou shalt give it unto the stranger that is in thy gates, that he may eat it; or thou mayest sell it unto an alien: for thou art an holy people unto the LORD thy God. Thou shalt not seethe a kid in his mother's milk.

Answer

Because God had called the Jews to be a peculiar people, they were to be a clean people. God said, "Now therefore, if ye will obey my voice indeed, and keep my covenant, then ye shall be a peculiar treasure unto me above all people: for all the earth is mine: And ye shall be unto me a kingdom of priests, and an holy nation" (Exodus 19:5, 6). Therefore, though in normal circumstances they were permitted to eat clean animals, when an animal died of itself they were not to touch it lest they become unclean (Leviticus 11:39, 40). However, these ceremonial rules did not pertain to non-Jews. As a result, they could sell the dead animals to the Gentiles without the Gentile being ceremonially unclean. Through the prophet Isaiah God admonished His people to, "Depart ye, depart ye, go ye out from thence, touch no unclean thing; go ye out of the midst of her; be ye clean, that bear the vessels of the LORD" (Isaiah 52:11). The reason for not seething a "kid in his mother's milk" was to avoid idolatry. This was a Canaanite practice of boiling sacrificial kids in their mother's milk as a heathen ritual.

Deuteronomy 14:26

And thou shalt bestow that money for whatsoever thy soul lusteth after, for oxen, or for sheep, or for wine, or for strong drink, or for whatsoever thy soul desireth: and thou shalt eat there before the LORD thy God, and thou shalt rejoice, thou, and thine household.

Answer

This counsel was given to the people at a time when they were yet wondering in the wilderness. The Lord said, "Thou shalt truly tithe all the increase of thy seed, that the field bringeth forth year by year. And thou shalt eat before the LORD thy God, in the place which he shall choose to place his name there" (Deuteronomy 14:22, 23). This counsel in particular applied to those who lived a long distance from the sanctuary (verse 24). They were to take their increase (produce, livestock, etc.), sell it, and "turn it into money" (verse 25). Then when they came near the tabernacle they were to buy with their tithe money whatever they desired to offer to the Lord (verse 26). Notice that verse three prohibited the eating of anything "abominable." So the phrase "whatsoever thy soul lusteth after " had its limitations. As pertaining to the strong drink, there were specific instructions concerning what should be done with it. Unfortunately, some have taken the wording "whatsoever thine soul lusteth after" as permission to imbibe alcoholic beverages. But the believer was not to drink the wine or strong drink. The command was, "And the drink offering thereof shall be the fourth part of an hin for the one lamb: in the holy place shalt thou cause the strong wine to be poured unto the LORD for a drink offering" (Numbers 28:7).

Deuteronomy 22:5

The woman shall not wear that which pertaineth unto a man, neither shall a man put on a woman's garment: for all that do so are abomination unto the LORD thy God.

Answer

This text has contributed to schisms in churches and religion in general. While in some cultures it is mandatory for men and women to wear specific clothing, in other parts of the world, especially in Western first-world countries, this mandate does not exist. The problem lies in the way some Christians interpret this text. Some insist that women should not wear pants, claiming that pants are men's clothing. Usually this verse is employed to address women. However, the text is not singular in gender. While it is true that prior to the early 1900s only men wore pants in Western societies, pants for women have become the norm. Though that is the case, women's slacks vary in style, and generally speaking are more feminine in appearance lending to only women wearing them. On the other hand, in biblical times men wore tunics—skirt-like garments that reached to the ankles. Ruth said to Boaz, "Spread therefore thy skirt over thine handmaid" (Ruth 3:9).

The pants issue is one that exists in some parts of the world, while in other parts (like China, Vietnam, etc.) pants are part of the common wear for women. In Scotland men wear kilts. It is a skirt reaching about the length of the knee made of pleated tartan cloth, traditionally worn by men as part of Scottish Highland dress. Girls and women now also wear it. Depending on the culture, distinctions are usually made in dress to distinguish between male and female.

This prohibition was probably made for several reasons. A distinction was intended. It was to avoid confusion between the sexes. Another probable reason was that in that day, as it is today in some parts of the world, there was a heathen custom of simulating a change of sex for immoral purposes. Men wore women's clothes and offered their bodies for immoral intentions. Another reason was that certain attire was intended for identification purposes. Such was the case with David's daughter. "And she had a garment of divers colours upon her: for with such robes were the king's daughters that were virgins appareled" (2 Samuel 13:8). This is interesting in as much as a man named Joseph had a "coat of many colours" (Genesis 37:3).

Caution should be taken relative to the enforcement of this verse from a chauvinistic perspective. Even Paul when dealing with the issue of hair on men or women said, "But if any man seem to be contentious, we have no such custom, neither the churches of God" (1 Corinthians 11:16).

Deuteronomy 23:18
Thou shalt not bring the hire of a whore, or the price of a dog, into the house of the LORD thy God for any vow: for even both these are abomination unto the LORD thy God.

Answer
The practice of the heathen was to make money off their daughters whom they caused to be prostitutes. This evil practice is still being carried out in many countries of the world. The Lord forbade this practice among His people. God said, "Do not prostitute thy daughter, to cause her to be a whore; lest the land fall to whoredom, and the land become full of wickedness" (Leviticus 19:29). Therefore, the Lord would not accept an offering of money gained from such vile practices. The word "dog" is a contemptuous term in Hebrew (1 Samuel 17:43; 2 Samuel 16:9). In this case, it is used to designate the person mentioned in verse 17 as a "Sodomite." In other words, do not bring to God money gained by the detestable practices of either male or female prostitution.

Judges 11:30,31
And Jephthah vowed a vow unto the LORD, and said, If thou shalt without fail deliver the children of Ammon into mine hands, Then it shall be, that whatsoever cometh forth of the doors of my house to meet me, when I return in peace from

*the children of Ammon, shall surely be the LORD'S, and I
will offer it up for a burnt offering.*

Answer

When I first read this, I became sick at heart. I just could not
believe that God would allow the father to carry through with
his vow and sacrifice his daughter. I later found out that many
people have this view. But taking a closer look at the context, I
was relieved with the answer. The solution is in the translation.
In most Bibles that have a marginal reference there is a number
next to the word "and" after "shall surely be the Lord's." The
actual word should be "or" in the place of "and." In other
words, she was dedicated to the service of God. The words
should read, "shall surely be the Lord's, or I will offer it up."
The offering of people to the Lord's service was common. In
the book of Numbers we read, "And thou shalt set the Levites
before Aaron, and before his sons, and offer them for an
offering unto the LORD. Thus shalt thou separate the Levites
from among the children of Israel: and the Levites shall be
mine. And after that shall the Levites go in to do the service
of the tabernacle of the congregation: and thou shalt cleanse
them, and offer them for an offering" (Numbers 8:13-15).

It is clear from this reading that the Levites were not offered
as human sacrifices, but rather that their lives were given
in service to the Lord. This girl "lamented her virginity,"
so the maidens went to visit her once a year. Since she
was dedicated to the service of the Lord, she apparently
never got married. This indeed was a great sacrifice for
women of those days. And since it was Jephthah's only
child, he would have no descendants to carry on his name.

1 Samuel 28:14

And he said unto her, What form is he of? And she said, An old man cometh up; and he is covered with a mantle. And Saul perceived that it was Samuel, and he stooped with his face to the ground, and bowed himself.

Answer

The Spirit of God had rejected Saul, the first king of Israel (1 Samuel 16:14). His awareness of his disconnection with God caused a dreadful terror. In his anxiety he crossed over the threshold of no return. His end is revealed in the following most awful words: "So Saul died for his trespass which he committed against Jehovah, because of the word of Jehovah, which he kept not; and also for that he asked counsel of one that had a familiar spirit, to inquire thereby, and inquired not of Jehovah: therefore he slew him, and turned the kingdom unto David the son of Jesse" (1 Chronicles 10:13,14). Turning one's back to the Spirit of God creates a vacuum to be filled with possessive and seducing spirits. Giving insight to this phenomena, Jesus said, "When the unclean spirit is gone out of a man, he walketh through dry places, seeking rest; and finding none, he saith, I will return unto my house whence I came out. And when he cometh, he findeth it swept and garnished. Then goeth he, and taketh to him seven other spirits more wicked than himself; and they enter in, and dwell there: and the last state of that man is worse than the first" (Luke 11:24-26).

The reasons why the apparition was not Samuel are the following:

1. God had departed from Saul and would not communicate with him (1 Samuel 28:15). And if God would not communicate with Saul through Samuel while he was yet alive, it would

be inconceivable that God would permit Samuel, even if it were possible, to communicate with him after his demise.

2. It would diametrically oppose every principle of righteousness to suppose that divine authority would be granted to a necromancer to act in the place of God, (who alone can resurrect the dead) to bring back Samuel from the dead.

3. God, who had condemned the practice of witchcraft (Deuteronomy 18:10-12), would not acquiescence to the request of a medium, and allow a righteous man to be manipulated by an agent of Satan.

4. The apparition was supposedly "brought up." Other expressions: "ascending out of the earth," "cometh up," and "bring ... up." This is not the habitation of the righteous dead — down in the earth. That is, if they are actually alive. Even those who believe in the immortal soul concord that the righteous are not down in the earth.

5. The apparition of Samuel told Saul, "Tomorrow shalt thou and the sons be with me." Saul had departed from God and committed suicide on the following day; Samuel was righteous. If Saul was to be with Samuel, then this raises the question: do the wicked and the righteous share the same abode? Do the wicked and the righteous dwell together? The answer is obvious. No!

6. This apparition was declaring the certainty of Saul's and his sons' death, which took place the next day (1 Samuel 31:2-6). Therefore, he was referring to death and the grave and not heaven.

7. Saul only perceived that it was Samuel based on the information he received from the witch, and only concluded that it was the old prophet from the description. The truth is that the devil,

through his medium, gave a description familiar to Saul, thus deceiving him. It was nothing more than a satanic séance.

8. Samuel is described as an old man. Obviously, for Samuel, death did not clothe him with the vigor of eternal youth, neither did a robe of righteousness get placed on him.

2 Samuel 7:15,16

But my mercy shall not depart away from him, as I took it from Saul, whom I put away before thee. And thine house and thy kingdom shall be established for ever before thee: thy throne shall be established for ever.

Answer

This promise, though apparently unconditional, failed because of the unfaithfulness of David's posterity (1 Kings 9:4-7). The last reigning descendant king of David's linage was Jehoiachin, who died in Babylon. In the days of Ezra and Nehemiah (during the reign of the Persian kings) there were no kings in Israel. From that time until the appearing of Christ, Israel was under the rule of pagan kings. And from the time of Christ until our day, Israel has had no king ruling. Therefore, the kingdom does not pertain to physical Israel, but spiritual Israel. This promise is fulfilled in the spiritual kingdom of Christ. "For unto us a child is born, unto us a son is given: and the government shall be upon his shoulder: and his name shall be called Wonderful, Counsellor, The mighty God, The everlasting Father, The Prince of Peace. Of the increase of his government and peace there shall be no end, upon the throne of David, and upon his kingdom, to order it, and to establish it with judgment and with justice from henceforth even for ever. The zeal of the LORD of hosts will perform this" (Isaiah 9:6,7). "Behold, the days come, saith the LORD, that I will raise unto

David a righteous Branch, and a King shall reign and prosper, and shall execute judgment and justice in the earth. In his days Judah shall be saved, and Israel shall dwell safely: and this is his name whereby he shall be called, THE LORD OUR RIGHTEOUSNESS" (Jeremiah 23:5, 6). The promise to David is fulfilled in Christ, whose kingdom is eternal. "The kingdoms of this world are become the kingdoms of our Lord, and of his Christ; and he shall reign for ever and ever" (Revelation 11:15).

The nation of literal Israel's house was left desolate and the kingdom was taken from them (Matthew 21:43) and given to another nation (Acts 13:46; 1 Peter 2:9, 10). Those who are looking for literal Israel to fulfill the promises of glory are looking in the wrong direction. The apostle Paul makes it plain that the true Israelites are those born again in Christ. "For he is not a Jew, which is one outwardly; neither is that circumcision, which is outward in the flesh: But he is a Jew, which is one inwardly; and circumcision is that of the heart, in the spirit, and not in the letter; whose praise is not of men, but of God." "Not as though the word of God hath taken none effect. For they are not all Israel, which are of Israel: Neither, because they are the seed of Abraham, are they all children: but, In Isaac shall thy seed be called. That is, They which are the children of the flesh, these are not the children of God: but the children of the promise are counted for the seed" (Romans 2:28,29; 9:6-8). To the Galatians he writes, "Know ye therefore that they which are of faith, the same are the children of Abraham. So then they which be of faith are blessed with faithful Abraham. There is neither Jew nor Greek, there is neither bond nor free, there is neither male nor female: for ye are all one in Christ Jesus. And if ye be Christ's, then are ye Abraham's seed, and heirs according to the promise" (Galatians 3:7, 9, 28-29). All who accept Christ are spiritual Israelites and heirs of the kingdom.

1 Kings 17:21, 22

And he stretched himself upon the child three times, and cried unto the LORD, and said, O LORD my God, I pray thee, let this child's soul come into him again. And the LORD heard the voice of Elijah; and the soul of the child came into him again, and he revived.

Answer

The prayer of the prophet is that the life (soul) of the boy return to him. The Hebrew word *nephesh* translated in this verse as "soul" appears in the Old Testament more than 700 times and is translated 117 times into English as "life." An example of *nephesh* translated "life" is found in 1 Kings 19:4, in which Elijah declares, "O Lord, take away my life [Heb. *nephesh*]." Another example of soul meaning life is recorded in the Psalms. "Let them be ashamed and confounded together that seek after my soul [Hebrew *nephesh*] to destroy it; let them be driven backward and put to shame that wish me evil" (Psalm 40:14). The translation "soul" in the verse in question can be misleading if taken as an immortal entity capable of a conscious existence when detached from the body. The Bible is emphatic when it says, "For the living know that they shall die: but the dead know not any thing, neither have they any more a reward; for the memory of them is forgotten. Also their love, and their hatred, and their envy, is now perished; neither have they any more a portion for ever in any thing that is done under the sun" (Ecclesiastes 9:5, 6). Never once in all the 700 times does this Hebrew word suggest or imply that a soul is immortal.

Nehemiah 9:14

And madest known unto them thy holy sabbath, and commandedst them precepts, statutes, and laws, by the hand of Moses thy servant.

Answer

This text does not imply that the Sabbath was first given by the hand of Moses: nor that precepts, statutes, and laws were first instituted by him. The fourth commandment begins with the words "Remember the Sabbath day" (Exodus 20:8). This admonition did not only suggest that it be not forgotten in the future, it also implied that it was already given. They were already keeping the Sabbath (when the manna was provided) prior to it being reiterated at Mt. Sinai (Exodus 16:23- 26). And centuries before, it was given and kept by the Creator and by the first parents (Genesis 2:2-4). And at least four hundred years prior to Mt. Sinai it was said of Abraham, "Because that Abraham obeyed my voice, and kept my charge, my commandments, my statutes, and my laws" (Genesis 26:5). What the text is saying is that Moses was the instructor used to give the instructions mentioned.

Job 14:21,22

His sons come to honour, and he knoweth it not; and they are brought low, but he perceiveth it not of them.
But his flesh upon him shall have pain,
and his soul within him shall mourn.

Answer

The answer to these verses is found in the poetic personification of inanimate objects. In Psalm 148:3-10 the Psalmist is ascribing to celestial orbs, animals, the elements of nature (snow, hail, etc.) and all matter the ability to feel gratitude as humans do, and express it in praises to the Lord. Job does the same thing. "But ask now the beasts, and they shall teach thee; and the fowls of the air, and they shall tell thee: Or speak to the earth, and it shall teach thee: and the fishes of the sea shall declare unto thee. Who knoweth not in all these that the hand of the LORD hath wrought this? In whose hand is the soul [*nephesh*] of every living thing, and the breath of all mankind" (Job 12:7-10). In the process of the unconscious state of a person succumbing to the effects of death, the body contorts. Thus Job is graphically relating the ravages of death, and in that condition his inability to sense anything around him. In death a father cannot see his sons honored, nor is he able to sympathize with their problems.

Job 34:14,15

If he set his heart upon man, if he gather unto himself his spirit and his breath; All flesh shall perish together, and man shall turn again unto dust.

Answer

The "he" of verse 14 is referring to God (verse 12), and what he has power to do. It was God who in the beginning "formed man of the dust of the ground, and breathed into his nostrils the breath of life; and man became a living soul" (Genesis 2:7).

Without the breath man could not live. Then when man sinned, God said, "In the sweat of thy face shalt thou eat bread, till thou return unto the ground; for out of it wast thou taken: for dust thou art, and unto dust shalt thou return" (Genesis 3:19). Notice that God clearly describes the habitat of man when he dies—not heaven, but dust. The parallelism used by Job of "breath" and "spirit" is used in Job 27:3: "All the while my breath is in me, and the spirit of God is in my nostrils." The same concept is found in the Psalms: "Thou hidest thy face, they are troubled: thou takest away their breath, they die, and return to their dust. Thou sendest forth thy spirit, they are created: and thou renewest the face of the earth" (Psalm 104:29,30).

In the book of Ezekiel the words "breath," and "spirit" are used interchangeably. Notice the wording. "Thus saith the Lord GOD unto these bones; Behold, I will cause breath to enter into you, and ye shall live: And I will lay sinews upon you, and will bring up flesh upon you, and cover you with skin, and put breath in you, and ye shall live; and ye shall know that I am the LORD" (Ezekiel 37:5-6). "Therefore prophesy and say unto them, Thus saith the Lord GOD; Behold, O my people, I will open your graves, and cause you to come up out of your graves, and bring you into the land of Israel. And ye shall know that I am the LORD, when I have opened your graves, O my people, and brought you up out of your graves, And shall put my spirit in you, and ye shall live, and I shall place you in your own land: then shall ye know that I the LORD have spoken it, and performed it, saith the LORD" (Ezekiel 37:12-14). Notice that in verses 5 and 6 the word "breath" is used, and in verses 12-14 the word "spirit" is used. Man can only live when the breath, or spirit, is given by God, the life-giver.

Proverb 16:4

The Lord has made all things for himself.
Yea, even the wicked for the day of evil.

Answer

From a surface reading this text appears to say that the wicked are made for destruction. Or as some people think: God created some people so He can destroy them. However, God did not create people to do evil, but rather created people who by their own volition have chosen to do evil. So in this sense He created the wicked. Having said that, there is a natural outcome for doing evil, just as there is a natural outcome for being righteous.

In other words, there are two roads (Matthew 7:13, 14): one leads to life, the other to destruction. Just as the wicked are not made for life ("for the wages of sin is death," Romans 6:23), so the righteous are not made for destruction ("the gift of God is eternal life," John 3:16). This does not mean that God purposefully created wicked people so He could destroy them. In the beginning it is said that God made everything "very good" (Genesis 1:31). There were only two righteous people created. The Scriptures does bear out that it is the devil that planted the wicked, while the Lord sowed the "good seed" (Matthew 13:25, 39). Therefore, this text has to be interpreted with these facts in mind.

Proverbs 31:6

Give strong drink unto him that is ready to perish,
and wine unto those that be of heavy hearts.

Answer

This verse has to be taken in the context of verses 4 and 5, which says, "It is not for kings to drink wine; nor for princes strong drink: Lest they drink, and forget the law, and pervert the judgment of any of the afflicted." Obviously, the counsel given before, "Wine is a mocker, strong drink is raging: and whosoever is deceived thereby is not wise" (Proverbs 20:1), explains why rulers should not imbibe. Because of the debilitating mental affect it was ill advisable for anyone in responsible positions to use fermented wine or strong drink. Take special notice that the use of alcoholic beverages perverts the good judgment of those that use it. And also, it leads them to forget the law, something that the writer of Proverbs considers unthinkable. For in chapter 28 he writes, "They that forsake the law praise the wicked: but such as keep the law contend with them." "He that turneth his ear from hearing the law, even his prayer shall be an abomination" (Proverbs 28:4, 9). In the next chapter he wrote, "Where there is no vision, the people perish:

but he that keepeth the law, happy is he" (Proverbs 29:18).

This suggestion is ironical in the sense that it suggests: if you're going to give strong drink to anyone, never give it to a ruler. Rather, give it to someone whose decision making has no impact on anyone. Apparently, in ancient times the only pain reducers were made of liquor mixed with certain drugs and given to people who were dying and in pain, or who had severe grief. During the crucifixion a mixture was given to convicts to lessen their agony. This was done to Christ: "They gave him vinegar to drink mingled with gall: and when he had tasted thereof, he would not drink" (Matthew 27:34). Christ's example of refusal eloquently testifies to the danger of mind-distorting drugs such as alcohol.

Isaiah 29:4

And thou shalt be brought down, and shalt speak out of the ground, and thy speech shall be low out of the dust, and thy voice shall be, as of one that hath a familiar spirit, out of the ground, and thy speech shall whisper out of the dust.

Answer

At first glance this appears to be talking about a person who dies. But when taking a closer look, it is clear that it is personifying Jerusalem. Because of Jerusalem's perfidious posture (in our modern terms two-timing) God declares its destiny. She would be humbled in the dust. Jerusalem is compared to a captured enemy groveling before his captor with his face in the dust and muttering vows of submission, in the hope of saving his life (see Lev. 19:31; Deut. 18:11). People that had familiar spirits muttered, or peeped. This was done by making unnatural, indistinct, and sonorous qualities of voice, such as might have been produced by speaking into a bottle or other receptacle. The possessor usually stooped while speaking as a medium, and according to Isaiah 29:4 spoke as if "out of the ground." The word translated "mutter" in Isaiah 8:19 means "to murmur," "to whisper," "to growl." The word translated "peep" is from *saphaph*, a word that imitates the mumbling of a medium. In Isaiah 29:4 *saphaph* is rendered "whisper," and in Isaiah 38:14, "chatter." So Jerusalem would be groveling in the ground making noises like one that had a familiar spirit.

Isaiah 35:9

No lion shall be there, nor any ravenous beast shall go up
thereon, it shall not be found there;
but the redeemed shall walk there.

Answer

In verse 4 the promise is, "Be strong, fear not: behold, your God will come with vengeance, even God with a recompense; he will come and save you." God will establish a new order, and when He does, nothing that "hurts or destroys" shall be there (Isaiah 11:6-9). The animal kingdom will be restored to its original state, when the lion was docile. "The wolf and the lamb shall feed together, and the lion shall eat straw like the bullock" (Isaiah 65:25).

Isaiah 45:7

I form the light, and create darkness: I make peace,
and create evil: I the LORD do all these things.

Answer

This text has troubled many who believe that it is the devil that brought about evil, not God (see Matthew 13:38, 39). However, the word "evil" is used in contrast to "peace." Another way to say it is that God can bring (peace) prosperity (Deuteronomy 23:6) as well as (evil) adversity. A cross-reference to this verse is found in Amos. "Shall a trumpet be blown in the city, and the people not be afraid? shall there be evil in a city, and the LORD hath not done it" (Amos 3:6).

Another cross-reference is found in 2 Chronicles 34:25-28. Notice verse 28. "Behold, I will gather thee to thy fathers, and thou shalt be gathered to thy grave in peace, neither shall thine eyes see all the evil that I will bring upon this place, and upon the inhabitants of the same. So they brought the king word again." It was the Lord that brought the plagues on Egypt. It is He that sometimes allows, or brings punishment to his children. (See Hebrews 12:6-11.) It was God that destroyed Sodom and Gomorrah while at the same time had mercy (or peace) on Lot and his family (Genesis 19:15-25). The same is true with the Flood. On Noah and his family He brought peace, while on the wicked disaster. The story of Rahab brings out the same outcomes. (See Joshua 6:20-25.) In the New King James version the word for "evil" is calamity.

Isaiah 65:20

There shall be no more thence an infant of days, nor an old man that hath not filled his days: for the child shall die an hundred years old; but the sinner being an hundred years old shall be accursed.

Answer

The phrase "no more thence an infant of days" suggests that premature death of an infant will not exist. There will be no such thing as "an old man that hath not filled his days." Then Isaiah uses the hyperbole "a child shall die an hundred years old." This phrase seems to be a contradiction of terms. But it is intended to make a point. Isaiah apparently makes an intentional deviation from a literal situation to embellish the picture he is painting of the new world. This is in contrast to there not being either an "infant of days," or "an old man." Generally speaking, a child is not one hundred years old. In verse 22 he states, "for as the days of a tree are the days of my people, and mine elect shall long enjoy the work of their hands" (Isaiah 65:22). All the figurative language is intended to make a contrast between what the people were experiencing and the hereafter. In the place of an infant of only days, he will be a child of a hundred years. Though the sinner in contrast may live a hundred years, he is worst off in that he is cursed and cut off from the mercy of God.

Isaiah 66:24

And they shall go forth, and look upon the carcases of the men that have transgressed against me: for their worm shall not die, neither shall their fire be quenched; and they shall be an abhorring unto all flesh.

Answer

Again, using hyperbole, Isaiah states that the "worm shall not die." This of course is in contrast to those carcases of people who have died. Their fire shall not "be quenched" is in contrast to the victims of the fire that are terminated by the fire. Isaiah is describing the final eradication of the wicked. The destroying elements will do and finish their work. In Psalm 91:8 God had promised, "Only with thine eyes shalt thou behold and see the reward of the wicked." At some point in the future before the complete consummation of the unrighteous this will transpire. But finally, all the wicked will desist. Zechariah 14:12 says, "Their flesh shall consume away while they stand upon their feet, and their eyes shall consume away in their holes, and their tongue shall consume away in their mouth." And Malachi 4:1, 3 says, "For, behold, the day cometh, that shall burn as an oven; and all the proud, yea, and all that do wickedly, shall be stubble: and the day that cometh shall burn them up, saith the LORD of hosts, that it shall leave them neither root nor branch. And ye shall tread down the wicked; for they shall be ashes under the soles of your feet in the day that I shall do this, saith the LORD of hosts."

The Psalmist declares: "For yet a little while, and the wicked shall not be: yea, thou shalt diligently consider his place, and it shall not be." "But the wicked shall perish, and the enemies of the LORD shall be as the fat of lambs: they shall consume; into smoke shall they consume away" (Psalm 37:10, 20). After the final annihilation of sinners, "wherein the heavens being on fire shall be dissolved, and the elements shall melt with fervent heat," God says, "Nevertheless we, according to his promise, look for new heavens and a new earth, wherein dwelleth righteousness" (2 Peter 3:12, 13).

Jeremiah 10:1-6

Hear ye the word which the LORD speaketh unto you, O house of Israel: 2 Thus saith the LORD, Learn not the way of the heathen, and be not dismayed at the signs of heaven; for the heathen are dismayed at them. 3 For the customs of the people are vain: for one cutteth a tree out of the forest, the work of the hands of the workman, with the axe. 4 They deck it with silver and with gold; they fasten it with nails and with hammers, that it move not. 5 They are upright as the palm tree, but speak not: they must needs be borne, because they cannot go. Be not afraid of them; for they cannot do evil, neither also is it in them to do good. 6 Forasmuch as there is none like unto thee, O LORD; thou art great, and thy name is great in might.

Answer

Some people have taken this text to mean that God forbids Christmas trees. While it is true that a tree is mentioned, the rest of the context clearly identifies what Jeremiah has been inspired to warn against. Idolatrous "customs of the people" are described as hewing down a tree, carving it, and shaping it into an idol. Then rearing it up, they decorate and venerate, or worship it. These graven images (verse 14) "cannot do evil, neither also is in them to do good" (verse 5). These idols will serve of no use or protection when the Lord comes. Isaiah writes, "And the loftiness of man shall be bowed down, and the haughtiness of men shall be made low: and the LORD alone shall be exalted in that day. And the idols he shall utterly abolish. And they shall go into the holes of the rocks, and into the caves of the earth, for fear of the LORD, and for the glory of his majesty, when he ariseth to shake terribly the earth. In that day a man shall cast his idols of silver, and his idols of gold, which they made each one for himself to worship, to the moles and to the bats" (Isaiah 2:17-20).

Jeremiah 17:27

But if ye will not hearken unto me to hallow the sabbath day, and not to bear a burden, even entering in at the gates of Jerusalem on the sabbath day; then will I kindle a fire in the gates thereof, and it shall devour the palaces of Jerusalem, and it shall not be quenched.

Answer

The thought that some take from this text is that there is a fire that never goes out. But the term "shall not be quenched" has to do with the work that the fire does, and while it is accomplishing its object, no one can quench it. Notice that the prophet Isaiah uses the same language: "And the streams thereof shall be turned into pitch, and the dust thereof into brimstone, and the land thereof shall become burning pitch. It shall not be quenched night nor day; the smoke thereof shall go up for ever: from generation to generation it shall lie waste; none shall pass through it for ever and ever. But the cormorant and the bittern shall possess it; the owl also and the raven shall dwell in it: and he shall stretch out upon it the line of confusion, and the stones of emptiness" (Isaiah 34:9-11). This prophecy pertaining to Idumea (Edom) speaks of it as a burning pitch that "shall not be quenched." Yet it speaks of different birds dwelling there. So, once the fire does its work then birds, not humans, will have their habitation there. This ancient area is now southern Israel and adjacent Jordan. This place is not still burning.

Jeremiah 31:15-17

Thus saith the LORD; A voice was heard in Ramah, lamentation, and bitter weeping; Rahel weeping for her children refused to be comforted for her children, because they were not. Thus saith the LORD; Refrain thy voice from weeping, and thine eyes from tears: for thy work shall be rewarded, saith the LORD; and they shall come again from the land of the enemy. And there is hope in thine end, saith the LORD, that thy children shall come again to their own border.

Answer

This prophecy was terribly fulfilled by Herod in Matthew 2:16-18, when he sought to destroy Christ. Parents have asked: Will children be saved in the kingdom? This is one promise that they shall be in the kingdom. The children were "from two years old and younger" (verse 16). Parents were not left hopeless, God made a promise! In the book of Isaiah, speaking of the new earth, it says, "and a little child shall lead (speaking of the animals) them … and a sucking child shall play on the hole of the asp, and the weaned child shall put his hand on the cockatrice den" (Isaiah 11:6-9). The children of Israel wandering in the desert were given this promise concerning their children: "Moreover your little ones, which ye said should be a prey, and your children, which in that day had no knowledge between good and evil, they shall go in thither, and unto them will I give it, and they shall possess it" (Deuteronomy 1:39). Jesus' own words attest to this hope. He said, "Suffer the little children to come unto me, and forbid them not: for of such is the kingdom of God" (Mark 10:14).

Ezekiel 16:11-13

I decked thee also with ornaments, and I put bracelets upon thy hands, and a chain on thy neck. And I put a jewel on thy forehead, and earrings in thine ears, and a beautiful crown upon thine head. Thus wast thou decked with gold and silver; and thy raiment was of fine linen, and silk, and broidered work; thou didst eat fine flour, and honey, and oil: and thou wast exceeding beautiful, and thou didst prosper into a kingdom.

Answer

This text is sometimes used to encourage the wearing of ornaments. However, it contradicts scores of texts in both the Old and New Testaments that discourage the use of ornaments worn by God's people. One such text reads, "And when the people heard these evil tidings, they mourned: and no man did put on him his ornaments. For the LORD had said unto Moses, Say unto the children of Israel, Ye are a stiffnecked people: I will come up into the midst of thee in a moment, and consume thee: therefore now put off thy ornaments from thee, that I may know what to do unto thee. And the children of Israel stripped themselves of their ornaments by the mount Horeb" (Exodus 33:4-6). In the New Testament, Peter wrote, "Whose adorning let it not be that outward adorning of plaiting the hair, and of wearing of gold, or of putting on of apparel; But let it be the hidden man of the heart, in that which is not corruptible, even the ornament of a meek and quiet spirit, which is in the sight of God of great price. For after this manner in the old time the holy women also, who trusted in God, adorned themselves, being in subjection unto their own husbands" (1 Peter 3:3-5). In both cases the wearing of ornaments is discouraged.

What then is the meaning? Obviously, there is no record that the Lord placed on each Israelite "a bracelet, a chain on the neck, earrings, and a beautiful crown." For among the Jews there were the poor. Those in better circumstances were admonished, "If thou lend money to any of my people that is poor by thee, thou shalt not be to him as an usurer, neither shalt thou lay upon him usury" (Exodus 22:25).

This language is figurative. When the Israelites were in Egypt, they were poor slaves. When God pulled them out of Egypt, he told them to borrow from the Egyptians. The Lord said, "Speak now in the ears of the people, and let every man borrow of his neighbour, and every woman of her neighbour, jewels of silver and jewels of gold. And the LORD gave the people favour in the sight of the Egyptians" (Exodus 11:2, 3). Then of all they had received, God commanded "Moses, saying, Speak unto the children of Israel, that they bring me an offering: of every man that giveth it willingly with his heart ye shall take my offering. And this is the offering which ye shall take of them; gold, and silver, and brass, And blue, and purple, and scarlet, and fine linen, and goats' hair, And rams' skins dyed red, and badgers' skins, and shittim wood, Oil for the light, spices for anointing oil, and for sweet incense, Onyx stones, and stones to be set in the ephod, and in the breastplate. And let them make me a sanctuary; that I may dwell among them" (Exodus 25:1-8). Israel was called the "church in the wilderness" (Acts 7:38). The sanctuary being the center of their worship was adorned as described in Ezekiel. God is speaking of His church as if it were a woman. After settling in Canaan, Solomon built a temple (replacing the old tabernacle) that aptly fits this description. (See 1 Kings 6:1-38.)

Ezekiel 36:25, 26

Then will I sprinkle clean water upon you, and ye shall be clean: from all your filthiness, and from all your idols, will I cleanse you. A new heart also will I give you, and a new spirit will I put within you: and I will take away the stony heart out of your flesh, and I will give you an heart of flesh.

Answer

This verse is reminiscent of the sanctuary services in the old tabernacle services. Concerning the Levites, Moses was commanded, "Take the Levites from among the children of Israel, and cleanse them. And thus shalt thou do unto them, to cleanse them: Sprinkle water of purifying upon them, and let them shave all their flesh, and let them wash their clothes, and so make themselves clean" (Numbers 8:6, 7). This symbolic cleansing was also done for lepers (Leviticus 14:7), those who touched dead bodies (Numbers 19:16-18), or a menstruous woman (Leviticus 15:19). All of these practices were part of the ceremonial services that were done away with at the cross.

"Neither by the blood of goats and calves, but by his own

blood he entered in once into the holy place, having obtained eternal redemption for us. For if the blood of bulls and of goats, and the ashes of an heifer sprinkling the unclean, sanctifieth to the purifying of the flesh: How much more shall the blood of Christ, who through the eternal Spirit offered himself without spot to God, purge your conscience from dead works to serve the living God?" (Hebrews 9:12-14). The sprinkling with the ashes of a heifer was included in the Old Testament (Numbers 19:17-19) and done away with in the New. It should be noted also that in Ezekiel, God is the one "sprinkling" and not man. Therefore, this text cannot be used to sanction sprinkling in the place of Bible baptism, which had to be done by immersion.

Amos 5:23

Take thou away from me the noise of thy songs;
for I will not hear the melody of thy viols.

Answer

There are churches that think it wrong to play musical instruments in their services. However, instruments were used in the sacred services of God in the Old Testament. Notice that David appointed singers and instruments. "And David spake to the chief of the Levites to appoint their brethren to be the singers with instruments of music, psalteries and harps and cymbals, sounding, by lifting up the voice with joy" (1 Chronicles 15:16). Solomon also "made of the almug trees pillars for the house of the LORD, and for the king's house, harps also and psalteries for singers: there came no such almug trees, nor were seen unto this day" (I Kings 10:12). The priest "did blow with the trumpets before the ark of God" (1 Chronicles 15:24). In the heavenly courts the twenty-four elders also use instruments. "And when he had taken the book, the four beasts and four and twenty elders fell down before the Lamb, having every one of them harps, and golden vials full of odours, which are the prayers of saints. And they sung a new song" (Revelation 5:8, 9). Those that use the text in question to forbid musical instruments in sacred service should consider that the prophet is speaking about "solemn assemblies" (verse 21) that had become detestable to God.

Amos 8:5

Saying, When will the new moon be gone, that we may sell corn? and the sabbath, that we may set forth wheat, making the ephah small, and the shekel great, and falsifying the balances by deceit?

Answer

There were apostates in Amos' day that were making a pretense of religion for their own gain. It was this state of being that prompted God to declare, "the end is come upon my people Israel" (verse 2). These mercenaries were anxious for the Sabbath to end so that they could sell their ware dishonestly, utilizing false balances. The "new moon" was the first day of the month (1 Samuel 20:5, 24, 27), and it was devoted to religious services. As a result, all trade was suspended. (See Numbers 28:11; 2 Kings 4:23.) This verse has nothing to do with the Sabbath permanently terminating, but rather when the religious day would end. This problem existed during the time of Nehemiah. He reminded the people of God in respect to their responsibilities in being faithful to him by obeying His precepts. He said, "And if the people of the land bring ware or any victuals on the sabbath day to sell, that we would not buy it of them on the sabbath, or on the holy day" (Nehemiah 10:31)

Sadly, there are those today that try to use this verse for the purpose of declaring that the Sabbath has ended. This is a stretch that cannot be supported at all from the context. It is the crooked, not God, that are greedily asking the question. They were anxious to take financial advantage of the people, which could not be done during religious activities.

Zechariah 14:16

And it shall come to pass, that every one that is left of all the nations which came against Jerusalem shall even go up from year to year to worship the King, the LORD of hosts, and to keep the feast of tabernacles.

Answer

This text is used to convince Christians that the Feast of Tabernacles should be kept in our day. The argument used is that since it will be kept in the kingdom, it should be kept today. But any Christian that urges others to observe the Jewish festivals is doing so in complete ignorance of Paul's writings concerning the feasts, or in obstinacy against his inspired counsels. In reference to the feasts Paul writes, "Blotting out the handwriting of ordinances that was against us, which was contrary to us, and took it out of the way, nailing it to his cross; And having spoiled principalities and powers, he made a shew of them openly, triumphing over them in it. Let no man therefore judge you in meat, or in drink, or in respect of an holyday, or of the new moon, or of the sabbath days: Which are a shadow of things to come; but the body is of Christ." "Having abolished in his flesh the enmity, even the law of commandments contained in ordinances." "Ye observe days, and months, and times, and years. I am afraid of you, lest I have bestowed upon you labour in vain" (Colossians 2:14-17; Ephesians 2:15; Galatians 4:10). It is clear from God's inspired New Testament writings that these feasts came to end in Christ. The handwriting of ordinances was written in the book of the law and was placed outside the ark of the testament. (See Deuteronomy 31:26). It was this law that was nailed to the cross. In Christ's life and ministry, there is no mention of him giving any special recognition to them.

First of all, this text is not referring to the Israelites observing the feast, but "everyone that is left of all the nations which came against Jerusalem ... whoso will not come up of all the families of the earth" (verse 17). These mentioned will "receive no rain," on top of that the "plague," and will be smitten (verse 18). "This shall be the punishment of Egypt, and the punishment of all nations that come not up to keep the feast of tabernacles" (verse 19). Obviously, to use this text to require a keeping of the feast for God's people today is to misuse it. No one believes nor teaches that upon the establishment of God's eternal kingdom there will still be unbelievers and heathens — people unwilling to worship Him. So what does the text mean?

This prophecy was conditional. The scriptures register several of them. For example, if there had been ten righteous in Sodom and Gomorrah the cities would have been spared (Genesis 18:32). Though Jonah preached Nineveh's destruction, the judgment against her was averted because she repented (Jonah 3:5-10). King Hezekiah was told he was going to die, but because of his pleading, God gave him fifteen more years (2 Kings 20:1, 5, 6). If the Israelites had kept themselves true to God and continued in the covenant, then what God is revealing in this text would have become a reality. The nations around Jerusalem would have been impressed with the godly state of Jerusalem and would have been drawn to Jehovah, the God of Israel, and kept the feast.

Malachi 4:5,6

Behold, I will send you Elijah the prophet before the coming of the great and dreadful day of the LORD: And he shall turn the heart of the fathers to the children, and the heart of the children to their fathers,
lest I come and smite the earth with a curse.

Answer

Elijah was one of two individuals in the entire Bible that did not see death (2 Kings 2:11). Enoch was the other (Genesis 5:21-24). Malachi's prediction has Elijah coming to "turn the heart of the fathers to the children," and vice versa. The question is: Was Elijah going to be reincarnated as some suppose? How would this prophecy be fulfilled? Reincarnation means that a person or animal dies and their soul is believed to be reborn in a different form. However, Elijah never died, so his soul (according to those who believe that the soul separates at death) could not have separated. So how is this riddle explained? The answer is found in the words of Christ. Speaking of John the Baptist, he said, "And from the days of John the Baptist until now the kingdom of heaven suffereth violence, and the violent take it by force. For all the prophets and the law prophesied until John. And if ye will receive it, this is Elias, which was for to come" (Matthew 11:12-14).

In addressing the role of John, Luke declared: "And many of the children of Israel shall he turn to the Lord their God. And he shall go before him in the spirit and power of Elias, to turn the hearts of the fathers to the children, and the disobedient to the wisdom of the just; to make ready a people prepared for the Lord" (Luke 1:16, 17). John's work was to be done in the "spirit and power" of Elijah. And again, before the Lord returns, the message will once more be given in the "spirit and power" of Elijah to prepare the way of the Lord's return.

NEW TESTAMENT

Matthew 3:10-12

And now also the axe is laid unto the root of the trees:
therefore every tree which bringeth not forth good fruit
is hewn down, and cast into the fire. I indeed baptize you
with water unto repentance: but he that cometh after me is
mightier than I, whose shoes I am not worthy to bear: he shall
baptize you with the Holy Ghost, and with fire: Whose
fan is in his hand, and he will throughly purge his floor,
and gather his wheat into the garner;
but he will burn up the chaff with unquenchable fire.

Answer

John the Baptist is the one addressing the crowd. Then speaking directly to the Pharisees he says: "Who hath warned you to flee from the wrath to come" (verse 7). John is speaking of two fires: one that purges from sin, and one that destroys the sinner. The first fire he mentions is from an analogy taken from Old Testament texts such as: "Therefore as the fire devoureth the stubble, and the flame consumeth the chaff, so their root shall be as rottenness, and their blossom shall go up as dust: because they have cast away the law of the LORD of hosts, and despised the word of the Holy One of Israel" (Isaiah 5:24). To the Israelites God said, "Understand therefore this day, that the LORD thy God is he which goeth over before thee; as a consuming fire he shall destroy them, and he shall bring them down before thy face: so shalt thou drive them out, and destroy them quickly, as the LORD hath said unto thee" (Deuteronomy 9:3). The other fire is used as a symbol of the purifying done by the Holy Ghost. Malachi says, "But who may abide the day of his coming? and who shall stand when he appeareth? for he is like a refiner's fire, and like fullers' soap: And he shall sit as a refiner and purifier of silver: and he shall purify the sons of Levi, and purge them as gold and silver, that they may offer unto the LORD an offering in righteousness" (Malachi 3:2, 3).

The prophet Isaiah records the two fires as well. "And I will turn my hand upon thee, and purely purge away thy dross, and take away all thy tin: And I will restore thy judges as at the first, and thy counsellors as at the beginning: afterward thou shalt be called, The city of righteousness, the faithful city. Zion shall be redeemed with judgment, and her converts with righteousness. And the destruction of the transgressors and of the sinners shall be together, and they that forsake the LORD shall be consumed" (Isaiah 1:25-28). The message is clear: Allow the Holy Spirit to purge away the sin, or the consuming fire will burn up the sinner. "Whose fan is in his hand, and he will throughly purge his floor, and will gather the wheat into his garner; but the chaff he will burn with fire unquenchable" (Luke 3:17).

Matthew 5:17

Think not that I am come to destroy the law, or the prophets: I am not come to destroy, but to fulfil.

Answer

This text has been used extensively by antinomians to suggest that by Christ fulfilling the law it makes it of none effect any longer. But Jesus' thought on the subject does not end with verse 17. He continues and says, "For verily I say unto you, Till heaven and earth pass, one jot or one tittle shall in no wise pass from the law, till all be fulfilled" (Matthew 5:18). Obviously, heaven and earth are still intact. Therefore, the law could not have passed. The problem with the misunderstanding is with the word "fulfill." However, if the rest of the chapter is read it becomes very obvious that Jesus is amplifying the law, not doing away with it. In fact, the word "fulfill" does not mean to "do away with," but rather to make full, make complete, or to meet its requirement. In Matthew, Jesus says to John the Baptist, "Suffer it to be so now: for thus it becometh us to fulfil all righteousness" (Matthew 3:15). If the word "fulfill" meant to terminate, it would then mean that Jesus is terminating all righteousness. This is not the case at all.

When Paul, Jesus' messenger to the Gentiles, was explaining how the law is fulfilled, he said, "Owe no man any thing, but to love one another: for he that loveth another hath fulfilled the law. For this, Thou shalt not commit adultery, Thou shalt not kill, Thou shalt not steal, Thou shalt not bear false witness, Thou shalt not covet; and if there be any other commandment, it is briefly comprehended in this saying, namely, Thou shalt love thy neighbour as thyself. Love worketh no ill to his neighbour: therefore love is the fulfilling of the law" (Romans 13:8-10). In Jesus' prayer, he prayed, "And now come I to thee; and these things I speak in the world, that they might have my joy fulfilled in themselves" (John 17:13). Jesus is not praying that their joy should end, but rather that his joy might be realized in them.

Matthew 5:19

Whosoever therefore shall break one of the least commandments, and shall teach men so, he shall be called the least in the kingdom of heaven: but whosoever shall do and teach them, the same shall be called great in the kingdom of heaven.

Answer

There are those who use this verse to assume that even if they violate the law of Christ they will still get into the kingdom, though being among the least. This word "least" in the Greek is: *elachstos* (elachistos). It is in reference to rank and excellence, or the lack thereof, of persons, or in the estimation of men.) As an adverb it refers to the smallest extent or degree; e.g. "turning up when he was least expected." It can be also used as an understatement, implying the reality is more extreme, usually worse e.g. "His performance was disappointing to say the least."

John the Baptist was called the least. But the word used in the Greek is *micros* (micros). It is in reference to size. This word is different in that it has to do with position and size as contrasting the word Jesus used in the text in question.

It should be noted that the text does not state that the person is in heaven, but rather that in heaven the offender is called "least." Jesus' words were pointing out how heaven dims a person. In Matthew chapter eighteen Jesus gave another example as to heaven's estimation, responding to the disciple's inquiry, "Who is the greatest in the kingdom of heaven?" (Matthew 18:1). Rephrasing the question, they asked, "In heaven's estimation who is considered the greatest?" He "called a little child unto him, and set him in the midst of them, And said, Verily I say unto you, Except ye be converted, and become as little children, ye shall not enter into the kingdom of heaven. Whosoever therefore shall humble himself as this little child, the same is greatest in the kingdom of heaven" (Matthew 18:2-4). In chapter five of Matthew, Jesus drives home the meaning: "For I say unto you, that except your righteousness shall exceed the righteousness of the scribes and Pharisees, ye shall in no case enter into the kingdom of heaven" (Matthew 5:20).

Matthew 10:28

And fear not them which kill the body, but are not able to kill the soul: but rather fear him which is able to destroy both soul and body in hell.

Answer

Those that teach that the soul is immortal have problems with this verse. Jesus' absolute statement is crystal clear — the soul can be destroyed. In fact, the prophet Ezekiel declares, "the soul that sinneth, it shall die" (Ezekiel 18:20). So what does the Lord mean? According to the Bible there are two deaths. The first one is the temporal death. Both good and bad people suffer this one. But the second one only the unrighteous suffer. This is the eternal or "second death." Jesus said, "He that overcometh shall not be hurt of the second death" (Revelation 2:11). This second death occurs in the lake of fire. "But the fearful, and unbelieving, and the abominable, and murderers, and whoremongers, and sorcerers, and idolaters, and all liars, shall have their part in the lake which burneth with fire and brimstone: which is the second death. Revelation 21:8.

According to the Revelator all the lost that are not in the book of life will be in that lake. "And death and hell were cast into the lake of fire. This is the second death. And whosoever was not found written in the book of life was cast into the lake of fire (Revelation 20:14, 15). Even the devil will not escape the flames of the second death. The Bible says, "And the devil that deceived them was cast into the lake of fire and brimstone" (Revelation 20:10). So while men can touch the physical body, only God has control over the entire fate or destiny of men. In the book of Luke he records these words of Jesus that shed more light on the subject: "And I say unto you my friends, Be not afraid of them that kill the body, and after that have no more that they can do. But I will forewarn you whom ye shall fear: Fear him, which after he hath killed hath power to cast into hell" (Luke 12:4, 5).

Matthew 12:31-32

Wherefore I say unto you, All manner of sin and blasphemy shall be forgiven unto men: but the blasphemy against the Holy Ghost shall not be forgiven unto men. And whosoever speaketh a word against the Son of man, it shall be forgiven him: but whosoever speaketh against the Holy Ghost, it shall not be forgiven him, neither in this world, neither in the world to come.

Answer

This text seems to make the Holy Spirit more prominent than Jesus. It appears that anything done against Christ will be forgiven, but speaking a word against the Holy Spirit is unpardonable. It should be stated here that the Lord promises to forgive. He says, "If we confess our sins, he is faithful and just to forgive us our sins, and to cleanse us from all unrighteousness" (1 John 1:9). The unpardonable sin is not murder, rape, or stealing. King David committed adultery (2 Samuel 12:9), Moses and Paul killed (Exodus 2:11, 12; Acts 26:10, 11; 1 Timothy 1: 13; 2 Timothy 1:12), and Peter cursed (Matthew 26:73, 74), but they repented and were forgiven.

What then is this sin? Paul addresses this issue in the book of Hebrews. He writes, "For it is impossible for those who were once enlightened, and have tasted of the heavenly gift, and were made partakers of the Holy Ghost, And have tasted the good word of God, and the powers of the world to come, if they shall fall away, to renew them again unto repentance; seeing they crucify to themselves the Son of God afresh and put him to an open shame" (Hebrews 6:4-6). The unpardonable sin is the constant resistance against the Holy Spirit. It was said of the Jews, "Ye stiffnecked and uncircumcised in heart and ears, ye do always resist the Holy Ghost: as your fathers did, so do ye" (Acts 7:51). It is the Spirit that brings conviction of sin, of righteousness, and of judgment (John 16:8). Without His aid, a person cannot repent. Without repentance, a person will not confess, and forsake sin. Without confession, there is no forgiveness. Paul further said, "For if we sin willfully after that we have received the knowledge of the truth, there remaineth no more sacrifice for sins, But a certain fearful looking for of judgment and fiery indignation, which shall devour the adversaries. He that despised Moses' law died without mercy under two or three witnesses: Of how much sorer punishment, suppose ye, shall he be thought worthy, who hath trodden under foot the Son of God, and hath counted the blood of the covenant, wherewith he was sanctified, an unholy thing, and hath done despite unto the Spirit of Grace" (Hebrews 10:26-29). This grievous sin is committed when a person is obstinate and willfully practices sin against his conscience. The time comes when the conscience becomes seared (1 Timothy 4:2). Hence, they become incapable of sensing the sweet voice of the Spirit's wooing. Like King Saul, they pass beyond the line of no return. (See 1 Samuel 10:9, 10; 16:14; 1 Chronicles 10:13, 14.) "He that covereth his sins shall not prosper: but whoso confesseth and forsaketh them shall have mercy" (Proverbs 28:13).

Matthew 12:40
For as Jonas was three days and three nights in the whale's belly; so shall the Son of man be three days and three nights in the heart of the earth.

Answer

One thing that can be said about this text is that our Lord and Savior believed that there was such a person in history as Jonah, and that he did survive the ordeal of being swallowed by the fish. The question is, What did Jesus mean by these words? Some take it to mean that Jesus would spend exactly three days and three nights (72 hours) in the grave. But no theory put forth so far has been able to prove this. It should be noted that of all the Gospel writers, Matthew is the only one in this instant that makes this statement. All the other times he and the other writers say, "the third day," "after three days," "in three days," "on the third day," and "after the third day" (Matthew 16:21; 17:22, 23; 27:63, 64; Mark 8:31; 9:31; 10:31; Luke 9:22; 11:30; 18:33). The key to this riddle is not on the precise amount of time, but rather on the miracle of rising again. Heretofore, no man had ever been able to raise himself back to life. Jesus proclaimed he could do it to prove beyond a shadow of a doubt that he was whom he claimed to be, "the divine Son of God." On the day of the resurrection the angel proclaimed, "He is not here: for he is risen, as he said" (Matthew 28:6). And in John 20:9 it says, "For as yet they knew not the scriptures, that he must rise again from the dead."

According to the scriptures Jesus resurrected just before dawn on the first day of the week (Matthew 28:1, Mark 16:9). The angel declared: "Saying, The Son of man must be delivered into the hands of sinful men, and be crucified, and the third day rise again" (Luke 24:7). It was on this "same day" (verse 13) that two disciples made their way to Emmaus. In response to Jesus' inquiry (not knowing that it was him), "they said unto him, Concerning Jesus of Nazareth, which was a prophet mighty in deed and word before God and all the people: And how the chief priests and our rulers delivered him to be condemned to death, and have crucified him. But we trusted that it had been he which should have redeemed Israel: and beside all this, to day is the third day since these things were done" (Luke 24:19-21). Notice that they clearly state, "today is the third day since these things were done." They include the condemnation, the crucifixion, and the resurrection of Christ. Then Jesus very clearly declares, "Thus it is written, and thus it behoved Christ to suffer, and to rise from the dead the third day" (Luke 24:46). If it were imperative to have Jesus in the grave for 72 hours, then he would have to be placed in the tomb on Thursday morning around 5:30 a.m., given that this is 72 hours backtracking from His resurrection. This does not make any sense. The only logical explanation is that of the Hebrew way of calculating time. Any part of a day is considered a day. (See Genesis 4:17-19; Esther 4:16; 5:1; 2 Chronicles 10:5, 12; 1 Kings 18:9, 10, 46.) Thus Jesus died on Friday, and then performed the greatest miracle ever for the hope of mankind–He resurrected on Sunday breaking the portals of the tomb!

Matthew 15:11

Not that which goeth into the mouth defileth a man; but that which cometh out of the mouth, this defileth a man.

Answer

Anytime there is a text like this that by itself seems to say one thing, it is imperative to check the context. Most people take this as a literal statement made by Jesus relative to food. But Peter said to the Lord, "Declare unto us this parable" (verse 15). The Jews were upset with Christ for violating the Jewish custom of washing the hands. They remonstrated with Him concerning His and the disciples' disregard for the practice. (See verses 2-8.) To the disciples' inquiry concerning the meaning of the parable, Jesus answered, "These are the things which defile a man: but to eat with unwashen hands defileth not a man" (Matthew 15:20). There are those that use verse 11 to say that Jesus cleansed all meats. The problem with that is that Peter himself, the one who asked the question, a few years later upon seeing a vision said to God, "Not so, Lord; for I have never eaten any thing that is common or unclean" (Acts 10:14). If Peter had the understanding that all things were clean, he would have erelong eaten unclean animals. Peter, who had learned directly from Christ, knew that there were things that indeed do defile. We should never forget that Jesus did not come to cleanse animals, he came to purify sinners.

The issue was this: The Jewish leaders were worried about their traditions (Mark 7:5) and exterior cleansing, while their interior was polluted with murderous thoughts. Inward defilement was what Christ was addressing. He said, "Howbeit in vain do they worship me, teaching for doctrines the commandments of men. For laying aside the commandment of God, ye hold the tradition of men, as the washing of pots and cups: and many other such like things ye do" (Mark 7:7, 8). They made tradition more important than the law of God. He said to them, "Full well ye reject the commandment of God, that ye may keep your own tradition" (verse 9). Then He gave the example of Corban (verses 10-13). Jesus was condemning hypocrisy and all the lists of evils these leaders were secretly practicing with washed hands. "For from within, [He said] out of the heart of men, proceed evil thoughts, adulteries, fornications, murders, Thefts, covetousness, wickedness, deceit, lasciviousness, an evil eye, blasphemy, pride, foolishness: All these evil things come from within, and defile the man" (Mark 7:21-23). Several years after Christ's encounter with this issue, James wrote in his epistle, "And the tongue is a fire, a world of iniquity: so is the tongue among our members, that it defileth the whole body, and setteth on fire the course of nature; and it is set on fire of hell" (James 3:6). Defilement was still an issue at least sixty years later when John, the last of the disciples (about A.D. 96), was told by the Lord, "And there shall in no wise enter into it [God's kingdom] any thing that defileth, neither whatsoever worketh abomination, or maketh a lie: but they which are written in the Lamb's book of life" (Revelation 21:27).

Matthew 16:18

And I say also unto thee, That thou art Peter,
and upon this rock I will build my church;
and the gates of hell shall not prevail against it.

Answer

Throughout the scriptures Jesus is compared to a "rock." In Deuteronomy 32:4 Moses says, "He is the Rock, his work is perfect: for all his ways are judgment: a God of truth and without iniquity, just and right is he." Hannah sang, "There is none holy as the LORD: for there is none beside thee: neither is there any rock like our God" (1 Samuel 2:2). The Psalmist declared, "The LORD is my rock … " "For who is God save the LORD? or who is a rock save our God?" (Psalm 18:2, 31). Paul testifies to this truth. He wrote, "And did all drink the same spiritual drink: for they drank of that spiritual Rock that followed them: and that Rock was Christ" (1 Corinthians 10:4). Peter himself testified that Christ is the Rock. He wrote, "Wherefore also it is contained in the scripture, Behold, I lay in Sion a chief corner stone, elect, precious: and he that believeth on him shall not be confounded. Unto you therefore which believe he is precious: but unto them which be disobedient, the stone which the builders disallowed, the same is made the head of the corner, And a stone of stumbling, and a rock of offence, even to them which stumble at the word, being disobedient:

whereunto also they were appointed" (1 Peter 2:6-8).

Those that take this text to state that Christ built His church upon Peter have no ground to stand on. First of all, the gates of hell did prevail against Peter when with cursing he denied the Lord. (See Matthew 26:69-75). Second, Peter was not the leader of the Christian church. It was James the brother of Jesus. (See Matthew 13:55; Galatians 1:19). It was this James that the apostles went to for counsel, and who presided over the Jerusalem counsels. (See Acts 12:17; 15:13-21; 21:18.) Peter made the confession, "Thou art the Christ, the Son of the living God" (verse 16). It was Peter that made this confession when Christ asked, "Whom do men say that I the Son of man am?" (verse 13). It was on this confession that Jesus stated, "on this rock I will build my church."

Matthew 16:19

And I will give unto thee the keys of the kingdom of heaven: and whatsoever thou shalt bind on earth shall be bound in heaven: and whatsoever thou shalt loose on earth shall be loosed in heaven.

Answer

Since Christ is the "Rock" of verse 18, how is this text of the keys explained? "Christ is the head of the church: and he is the saviour of the body" (Ephesians 5:23). The body of Christ is the church on earth. "And hath put all things under his feet, and gave him to be the head over all things to the church, which is his body" (Ephesians 1:22, 23). To the church Christ has given certain responsibilities. One of those is to speak His words. It is the "words" that are the "keys" given to the church. Based on the Word, there is authority. Jesus said, "The words that I speak unto you, they are spirit, and they are life"

(John 6:63). Concerning the same episode of Matthew 16, John records these words: "Then Simon Peter answered him, Lord, to whom shall we go? thou hast the words of eternal life. And we believe and are sure that thou art that Christ, the Son of the living God" (John 6:68, 69). In His prayer Jesus said, "For I have given unto them the words which thou gavest me" (John 17:8). It is through the preaching of the word that people's sins are remitted. On the day of Pentecost these are the very words of Peter when under conviction the people asked, "men and brethren what shall we do?" (Acts 2:37). Peter responded and said, "Repent, and be baptized every one of you in the name of Jesus Christ for the remission of sins, and ye shall receive the gift of the Holy Ghost" (verse 38). Notice that Peter did not say, "I will remit your sins." Instead, it was by responding to the Word, by repenting, and being baptized that their sins would be remitted. Jesus referred to the knowledge of the truth as the "key." "Woe unto you, lawyers! for ye have taken away the key of knowledge: ye entered not in yourselves, and them that were entering in ye hindered." (Luke 11:52).

Matthew 16:28

Verily I say unto you, There be some standing here, which shall not taste of death,
till they see the Son of man coming in his kingdom.

Answer

The apostle Peter explains this verse. He wrote, "For we have not followed cunningly devised fables, when we made known unto you the power and coming of our Lord Jesus Christ, but were eyewitnesses of his majesty. For he received from God the Father honour and glory, when there came such a voice to him from the excellent glory, This is my beloved Son, in whom I am well pleased. And this voice which came from heaven we heard, when we were with him in the holy mount" (2 Peter 1:16-18). The words of Christ came true on the Mount of Transfiguration (Matthew 17:1-5). Notice that Peter uses the terms "coming of our Lord ... and were eyewitnesses of his majesty." That the disciples died and did not see His literal kingdom is clear. The Lord himself, after the resurrection, in response to the question, "Lord, wilt thou at this time restore again the kingdom to Israel?" (Acts 1:6), said to them, "It is not for you to know the times or the seasons, which the Father hath put in his own power" (verse 7). Jesus' promise to them: "Let not your heart be troubled: ye believe in God, believe also in me. In my Father's house are many mansions: if it were not so, I would have told you. I go to prepare a place for you. And if I go and prepare a place for you, I will come again, and receive you unto myself; that where I am, there ye may be also" (John 14:1-3). That's when they will see the actual kingdom!

Matthew 18:18

Verily I say unto you, Whatsoever ye shall bind on earth shall be bound in heaven: and whatsoever ye shall loose on earth shall be loosed in heaven.

Answer

The problem of keeping order in the church was committed to the church, not to an individual. Verse 18 follows the advice just given: "Moreover if thy brother shall trespass against thee, go and tell him his fault between thee and him alone: if he shall hear thee, thou hast gained thy brother. But if he will not hear thee, then take with thee one or two more, that in the mouth of two or three witnesses every word may be established. And if he shall neglect to hear them, tell it unto the church: but if he neglect to hear the church, let him be unto thee as an heathen man and a publican" (Matthew 18:15-17). Disorderly members were to be dealt with in the spirit and love of Christ. However, if after appropriate appeals no reconciliation was possible, then the church was to act by putting the member out of its fellowship. This action was to be carried out by the church on earth, and would be ratified in heaven. Paul, having an understanding of this, counseled the church at Corinth: "But now I have written unto you not to keep company, if any man that is called a brother be a fornicator, or covetous, or an idolater, or a railer, or a drunkard, or an extortioner; with such an one no not to eat. For what have I to do to judge them also that are without? do not ye judge them that are within? But them that are without God judgeth. Therefore put away from among yourselves that wicked person" (1 Corinthians 5:11-13). The opposite is true as well. The Bible says, "And the Lord added to the church daily such as should be saved" (Acts 2:47).

Matthew 22:31, 32

But as touching the resurrection of the dead, have ye not read that which was spoken unto you by God, saying, I am the God of Abraham, and the God of Isaac, and the God of Jacob? God is not the God of the dead, but of the living.

Answer

The Lord is addressing the Sadducees. This branch of priests did not believe in the resurrection of the dead. "For the Sadducees say that there is no resurrection, neither angel, nor spirit: but the Pharisees confess both" (Acts 23:8). One of the reasons contributing to this error was another error of only believing in the five books of Moses and nothing else. Had they accepted the rest of the Scriptures as inspired, they would have believed in the raising of the dead, for several resurrections are recorded there. There was the resurrection of the Shunammite woman's son (2 Kings 4:18-37). The dead man cast upon Elisha's bones

(2 Kings 13:20, 21). Job believed it (Job 19:24-26). Isaiah also wrote about it (Isaiah 26:19). The great vision of the dry bones was another Old Testament illustration (Ezekiel 37:1-14).

Since they did not accept the rest of the Old Testament as inspired, Jesus cited the reality from Moses' writings. He spoke about Abraham, Isaac, and Jacob being alive, because as far as He was concerned they would rise again. He said, "And I say unto you, That many shall come from the east and west, and shall sit down with Abraham, and Isaac, and Jacob, in the kingdom of heaven. But the children of the kingdom shall be cast out into outer darkness: there shall be weeping and gnashing of teeth" (Matthew 8:11, 12). In Luke 20:37 He is quoted as saying, "Now that the dead are raised, even Moses shewed at the bush, when he calleth the Lord the God of Abraham, and the God of Isaac, and the God of Jacob." To God, all who have loved Him are considered to be asleep, awaiting the great day of the resurrection. God has promised, "Thy dead men shall live, together with my dead body shall they arise. Awake and sing, ye that dwell in dust: for thy dew is as the dew of herbs, and the earth shall cast out the dead" (Isaiah 26:19).

Matthew 22:40
*On these two commandments
hang all the law and the prophets.*

Answer
Someone said to me that the only two commandments required for believers today are "Thou shalt love the Lord thy God with all thy heart, and with all thy soul, and with all thy mind. This is the first and great commandment. And the second is like unto it, Thou shalt love thy neighbour as thyself " (Matthew 22:37-39). This summary of the Ten

Commandments is just that, a summary! The term "hang," is the key to understanding this text. It means "suspend from" or "summed up." It is like saying, "It helps the picture to hang together." This does not do away with the picture. Instead, without it, the picture would fall apart. In other words, the summary of the Ten Commandments is love. Without love, an attempt to keep the law would be pure drudgery. That is why John wrote, "For this is the love of God, that we keep his commandments: and his commandments are not grievous" (1 John 5:3). Jesus said, "If you love me, keep my commandments. In His ministry when dealing with this topic, He always placed the commandments at the highest level. When asked by the rich young ruler, "What good thing shall I do, that I may have eternal life?" (Matthew 19:16). Jesus simply said, "If thou wilt enter into life, keep the commandments!" (verse 17). When asked which, He did not say, "Love the Lord." Instead, he mentioned a few of the commandments to clarify the fact that he was thinking of the Ten Commandments. (See verses 18, 19.)

The apostle Paul does the same thing in the letter to the Romans a few years after the cross. He wrote, "Owe no man any thing, but to love one another: for he that loveth another hath fulfilled the law. For this, Thou shalt not commit adultery, Thou shalt not kill, Thou shalt not steal, Thou shalt not bear false witness, Thou shalt not covet; and if there be any other commandment, it is briefly comprehended in this saying, namely, Thou shalt love thy neighbour as thyself. Love worketh no ill to his neighbour: therefore love is the fulfilling of the law" (Romans 13:8-10). Yes, love is revealed through the working out of the principles of the Ten Commandments in the life. As James rightly stated, "Even so faith, if it hath not works, is dead, being alone. Yea, a man may say, Thou hast faith, and I have works: shew me thy faith without thy works, and I will shew thee my faith by my works" (James 2:17, 18).

Matthew 25:46

And these shall go away into everlasting punishment:
but the righteous into life eternal.

Answer

There is a great difference between "punishment" and "punishing." A person who suffers capital punishment is not subject to continued punishing or continued suffering. This punishment mentioned by Jesus is "everlasting." There is a contrast here between "eternal life" — the reward of the righteous — and "everlasting punishment" — the destruction of the unrighteous. In fact, Paul says, "The wages of sin is death" (Romans 6:23), not eternal living in hell. Paul further declares, "Who shall be punished with everlasting destruction from the presence of the Lord, and from the glory of his power" (2 Thessalonians 1:9). In other words, the destruction is final, its results are everlasting; there is no reversal from its completed work.

Matthew 28:1

In the end of the sabbath, as it began to dawn toward
the first day of the week, came Mary Magdalene
and the other Mary to see the sepulchre.

Answer

This text on the surface seems to indicate that Christ rose on Sabbath afternoon. Though this verse seems to imply that, there are other Gospel writers that clarify the issue. In Mark 16 we read:

"And very early in the morning the first day of the week, they came unto the sepulchre at the rising of the sun." "Now when Jesus was risen early the first day of the week, he appeared first to Mary Magdalene, out of whom he had cast seven devils" (Mark 16:2, 9). Notice that Mark is describing the same women, and what transpired. These women are recorded in Luke as those "which came with him from Galilee, followed after, and beheld the sepulchre, and how his body was laid" (Luke 23:55). Then because of the lateness of the hour, since the Sabbath was about to begin, they "returned, and prepared spices and ointments; and rested the Sabbath day according to the commandment" (Luke 23:56). They could not have been there on the Sabbath, for it was holy to them. The "dawn" of this verse in question does not take place on Sabbath afternoon before sunset. Dawn occurs before daybreak.

The problem lies in the division of the verses between verse 66 of chapter 27 and verse one of chapter 28. The phrase, "in the end of the Sabbath" belongs to the preceding verse. The Jewish leaders, in order to guarantee that the Savior's word could not be fulfilled, went to Pilate late Sabbath afternoon. This took place after the preparation day, which is Friday. The record says, "Now the next day, that followed the day of the preparation, the chief priests and Pharisees came together unto Pilate, Saying, Sir, we remember that that deceiver said, while he was yet alive, After three days I will rise again. Command therefore that the sepulchre be made sure until the third day, lest his disciples come by night, and steal him away, and say unto the people, He is risen from the dead: so the last error shall be worse than the first. Pilate said unto them, Ye have a watch: go your way, make it as sure as ye can. So they went, and made the sepulchre sure, sealing the stone, and setting a watch" (Matthew 27:62-66).

Note that they were concerned that at "night" the disciples would come and steal the body. Therefore, the tomb was sealed before sunset on the Sabbath. Therefore, it would not have been possible for the woman to be there on the Sabbath.

The soldier's made-up story after the resurrection, suggested by the Jewish leaders, confirms that during the night the watch was kept after the Sabbath (Matthew 28:11-14). Since they kept watch through the night, the logical conclusion is what the Bible says: Jesus rose on the "first day of the week," not on Sabbath afternoon. The verse then should read, "So they went, and made the sepulchre sure, sealing the stone, and setting a watch in the end of the Sabbath. As it began to dawn toward the first day of the week, came Mary Magdalene and the other Mary to see the sepulchre" (Matthew 27:66; 28:1). This matches perfectly the testimony of all the other Gospel writers. (See Luke 24:1-46; John 20:1-19).

Luke writes, "Now upon the first day of the week, very early in the morning, they came unto the sepulchre, bringing the spices which they had prepared, and certain others with them." Then in verse 13 he says, "And, behold, two of them went that same day to a village called Emmaus, which was from Jerusalem about threescore furlongs." Notice that on the "same day" they took their journey. Then they state, "But we trusted that it had been he which should have redeemed Israel: and beside all this, to day is the third day since these things were done." Notice again that the first day of the week, or Sunday, is the "third day." Then Jesus himself confirms this fact. "And said unto them, Thus it is written, and thus it behoved Christ to suffer, and to rise from the dead the third day" (Luke 24:1, 13, 21, 46).

Mark 4:11,12

And he said unto them, Unto you it is given to know the mystery of the kingdom of God: but unto them that are without, all these things are done in parables: That seeing they may see, and not perceive; and hearing they may hear, and not understand; lest at any time they should be converted, and their sins should be forgiven them.

Answer

It appears from this statement that Christ is making it almost impossible for a certain group of people to see the light and be converted. But in the book of Matthew we get a better picture as to what was really taking place. "For this people's heart is waxed gross, and their ears are dull of hearing, and their eyes they have closed; lest at any time they should see with their eyes, and hear with their ears, and should understand with their heart, and should be converted, and I should heal them" (Matthew 13:15). The martyr Stephen stressed the same point that led to the same consequences as his Lord. He said, "Ye stiffnecked and uncircumcised in heart and ears, ye do always resist the Holy Ghost: as your fathers did, so do ye. Which of the prophets have not your fathers persecuted? and they have slain them which shewed before of the coming of the Just One; of whom ye have been now the betrayers and murderers: Who have received the law by the disposition of angels, and have not kept it. When they heard these things, they were cut to the heart, and they gnashed on him with their teeth" (Acts 7:51-54). Jesus well understood the heart of men. He said, "For every one that doeth evil hateth the light, neither cometh to the light, lest his deeds should be reproved. But he that doeth truth cometh to the light, that his deeds may be made manifest, that they are wrought in God" (John 3:20, 21).

The Lord has no pleasure in seeing anyone lost. "Therefore I will judge you, O house of Israel, every one according to his ways, saith the Lord GOD. Repent, and turn yourselves from all your transgressions; so iniquity shall not be your ruin. Cast away from you all your transgressions, whereby ye have transgressed; and make you a new heart and a new spirit: for why will ye die, O house of Israel? For I have no pleasure in the death of him that dieth, saith the Lord GOD:

wherefore turn yourselves, and live ye" (Ezekiel 18:30-32). "As I live, saith the Lord GOD, I have no pleasure in the death of the wicked; but that the wicked turn from his way and live: turn ye, turn ye from your evil ways; for why will ye die, O house of Israel?" (Ezekiel 33:11). And Peter, who was present when the Lord spoke these words, says, "The Lord is not slack concerning his promise, as some men count slackness; but is longsuffering to us-ward, not willing that any should perish, but that all should come to repentance" (2 Peter 3:9). From these verses it becomes quite obvious that the inability to see was not on the Lord's part, but rather on the hearers.

Mark 7:15

There is nothing from without a man, that entering into him can defile him: but the things which come out of him, those are they that defile the man.

Answer

See my comments on Matthew 15:11.

Mark 9:43, 44

And if thy hand offend thee, cut it off: it is better for thee to enter into life maimed, than having two hands to go into hell, into the fire that never shall be quenched:
Where their worm dieth not, and the fire is not quenched.

Answer

In the days of Christ there were two places where people could be buried. One was the typical grave called *hades*, where people who could afford it were buried. The other was the local city dump just outside Jerusalem. It was called *gehenna* in the Greek. This was the name for the valley of Hinnom. Criminals that had been crucified and were still alive were cast over the cliff into this burial place. There along with the city refuse and dead animals they would die of exposure or the wounds, or both. This garbage dump was always smoldering, and what was not consumed by the fire was devoured by the maggots. The Lord is using this place of continual burning as an illustration of total destruction. The idea of unquenchable fire is that the fire, not the victim, is unquenchable. This is the case with Jerusalem. God said, "Behold, mine anger and my fury shall be poured out upon this place, upon man, and upon beast, and upon the trees of the field, and upon the fruit of the ground; and it shall burn, and shall not be quenched" (Jeremiah 7:20). The fulfillment of the prophecy is recorded in the book of Chronicles. "And they burnt the house of God, and brake down the wall of Jerusalem, and burnt all the palaces thereof with fire, and destroyed all the goodly vessels thereof. And them that had escaped from the sword carried he away to Babylon; where they were servants to him and his sons until the reign of the kingdom of Persia" (2 Chronicles 36:19-20). Jerusalem, though burnt down, was rebuilt after the Jews returned back from the Babylonian captivity. (See Ezra 5:2; Haggai 1:14, 15.)

This text in question cannot be used as some try to, to support the doctrine of an immortal soul. Those who teach that doctrine teach that the soul is disembodied. The text contradicts that notion, for it mentions a body that worms eat. The idea is that "death shall feed on them" (Psalm 49:14). Therefore it is the entire person that is cast into hell. The Psalmist declares, "But the wicked shall perish, and the enemies of the LORD shall be as the fat of lambs: they shall consume; into smoke shall they consume away" (Psalm 37:20). Christ affirms the truth that it is the entire person. He said, "And if thy right hand offend thee, cut it off, and cast it from thee: for it is profitable for thee that one of thy members should perish, and not that thy whole body should be cast into hell" (Matthew 5:30).

Luke 9:60

Jesus said unto him, Let the dead bury their dead:
but go thou and preach the kingdom of God.

Answer

Christ, by this language, is seeking to impress this would-be follower of the prominence and urgency that the preaching of the gospel must have in order to follow Him. The responsibility of burying the dead in Oriental lands, even today, is considered one of the most sacred duties devolving upon a son. If this duty was considered extremely obligatory, then the preaching of the gospel to the living was even more essential. There is nothing that can be done for the deceased but to bury them. But there is much that can be done for those yet alive. Christ is not suggesting that the physically dead can do anything, for he inspired the writer of Ecclesiastes to write, "Whatsoever thy hand findeth to do, do it with thy might; for there is no work, nor device, nor knowledge, nor wisdom, in the grave, whither thou goest" (Ecclesiastes 9:10). The point is that others can do the mundane things while the follower has far more important things to do. In other words, what sacrifices are the would-be followers willing to make in order to follow Him?

Christ is relegating this responsibility to the spiritually dead. The apostle Paul speaks about being spiritually dead. "And you hath he quickened, who were dead in trespasses and sins; Wherein in time past ye walked according to the course of this world, according to the prince of the power of the air, the spirit that now worketh in the children of disobedience: Among whom also we all had our conversation in times past in the lusts of our flesh, fulfilling the desires of the flesh and of the mind; and were by nature the children of wrath, even as others. But God, who is rich in mercy, for his great love wherewith he loved us, Even when we were dead in sins, hath quickened us together with Christ, (by grace ye are saved;) And hath raised us up together, and made us sit together in heavenly places in Christ Jesus" (Ephesians 2:1-6). The word "quickened" means to be made alive. Those who are alive physically, but dead spiritually, are made alive by Christ to labor for him, and make whatever sacrifices to save the living lost.

Luke 15:22
But the father said to his servants, Bring forth the best robe, and put it on him; and put a ring on his hand, and shoes on his feet.

Answer

I have come across several folk that have used this text to justify the wearing of jewelry by Christians. Christ in this chapter cited three parables. Each has a message — the lost can be found! The parables are symbolic of the love that God has for the lost, and the sacrifice and resulting joy that comes when one is found and restored. "I say unto you, that likewise joy shall be in heaven over one sinner that repenteth, more than over ninety and nine just persons, which need no repentance" (verse 7). The backsliding son returns home after wasting his substance, and likewise joy erupts over his restoration. Just as the shepherd that finds the sheep, and the woman the lost coin, are allegorical, so is the story of the prodigal son. The shoes, coat, and ring were evidence of the boy being restored back into the family with all rights and privileges. Therefore, this text should not be employed for either killing the fatted calf, giving of a coat, or giving of rings.

I know of no church that uses this story to give every backslider a ring for coming back into the church; nor do they kill the fatted calf, or even give a coat. All who are acquainted with the scriptures know that a "coat" can be symbolic of the righteousness of Christ (Zechariah 3:1-7), the ring as a signet of authority (Esther 3:10; 8:2), and the shoes a symbol of being able to do business. "Now this was the manner in former time in Israel concerning redeeming and concerning changing, for to confirm all things; a man plucked off his shoe, and gave it to his neighbour: and this was a testimony in Israel. Therefore the kinsman said unto Boaz, Buy it for thee. So he drew off his shoe" (Ruth 4:7, 8). Clearly, this parable is given as an encouragement to the lost, that they can be restored, even if at one point a believer turns from the way.

Luke 16:16

The law and the prophets were until John: since that time the kingdom of God is preached, and every man presseth into it.

Answer

After the resurrection of Christ, He showed himself on several different occasions. One of these was to two disciples on the road to Emmaus. After questioning them He said, "O fools, and slow of heart to believe all that the prophets have spoken: Ought not Christ to have suffered these things, and to enter into his glory? And beginning at Moses and all the prophets, he expounded unto them in all the scriptures the things concerning himself " (Luke 24:25-27). Then He went and met with His disciples and said, "These are the words which I spake unto you, while I was yet with you, that all things must be fulfilled, which were written in the law of Moses, and in the prophets, and in the psalms, concerning me. Then opened he their understanding, that they might understand the scriptures" (verses 44 and 45). The phrase "Moses" is referring to the first five books of the Bible. In

German, and some other languages, the first five books are referred to as the first, second, third, fourth, and fifth books of Moses. The term "all the prophets" includes the rest of the writings of the prophets in the Old Testament.

The Lord demonstrated that everything that happened to Him was prophesied in the Old Testament. It is transparently clear that neither Jesus nor any of His apostles believed that the Old Testament was done away with. That is why Paul says, "All scripture is given by inspiration of God" (2 Timothy 3:16). The only scriptures available to the believers of those days were found in the Old Testament. It is also important to remember that Jesus said, "had ye believed Moses, ye would have believed me: for he wrote of me. But if ye believe not his writings, how shall ye believe my words? (John 5:46, 47). In this statement "the law and the prophets were until John" simply meant that the Old Testament pointed to John (Mark 1:1-8; Luke 3:4-6), and since that time Jesus took over the spreading of the gospel.

Luke 16:22, 23

And it came to pass, that the beggar died, and was carried by the angels into Abraham's bosom: the rich man also died, and was buried; And in hell he lift up his eyes, being in torments, and seeth Abraham afar off, and Lazarus in his bosom.

Answer

I had a man confront me and insist that the Bible taught an eternal, fiery hell with people in it. I asked him to produce the text. He referred to the text in question. But the question is whether this is a literal story or a parable. The Jews had accepted the Greek pagan idea of a fire after death that purifies the soul. Jesus took their erroneous idea and used it as a parable. First, He has the wretched poor man go up; in the Jewish concept, the poor were sinners deserving the flames. The rich man was sent to the place of burning, which in Jewish thought his riches gave evidence of his closeness to God, and should have gone up. The poor man is said to have gone to Abraham's bosom. No one believes that the saved go to Abraham's chest, else his chest must be humongous. So this is symbolic language. There are other points that concretely establish this as a parable, and thus must be symbolic:

1. The rich man "was buried" (verse 22). No one believes that the grave is a burning hell.

2. The rich man could talk directly to Abraham, thus placing heaven and hell in very close proximity (verse 23).

3. The rich man asked to have a drop of water placed on his tongue to cool him off. If this scene represents hell, then it must not be a very hot place (verse 24).

4. The request is not for Abraham but rather the beggar to get the cooling drop of water (verse 24). Can the saved visit those in hell? No one believes this either.

5. The reason stated for the rich man being in the place of torment is simply that while alive, he received "good things." On the other hand, Lazarus, because he received "evil things" while living now is "comforted." The Bible does not teach that people who get good things while alive are then punished when they die. If this were the case, then Abraham should be alongside the rich man, for he was very rich.

The message of Christ through this parable is that at death there is a great gulf fixed. There is no reversal of people's fate (verse 26). He also brought out the importance of having faith based on the Scriptures (Moses and the prophets), and not on miracles (verses 29 and 31). He is emphatic! They have "Moses and the Prophets; if they hear not them, neither will they be persuaded though one rose from the dead." It is interesting that Jesus did resurrect Lazarus, and they still did not believe as Jesus predicted (John 12:10, 11).

Luke 17:34-36

I tell you, in that night there shall be two men in one bed; the one shall be taken, and the other shall be left. Two women shall be grinding together; the one shall be taken, and the other left. Two men shall be in the field; the one shall be taken, and the other left.

Answer

Recently a lot of attention has been given to this text. It is viewed as supporting the rapture theory. However, a careful look at the context reveals no support for the idea. Jesus is speaking to His disciples and is using the "days of Noah" as a warning. He is not saying, "you better watch out, or you will be taken to heaven!" Rather, He is warning, "you better watch out or the same thing that happened to those in Noah's day will happen to you." They were "taken" by the Flood to destruction. In Matthew it says they were "taken," in Luke it says, "destroyed." Jesus then says, "As the days of Noe were, so shall also the coming of the Son of man be (verse 37). After the destruction takes place, He repeats the same, "so shall also the coming of the Son of man be" (verse 39). Christ is emphatic that the same thing will happen when He comes as transpired in Noah's day. The focus then is not on what happens to the righteous, but rather what happens to the unbelievers. Noah in Matthew and Lot in Luke 17:28-30 are only used as historical points of references, not for what happens to them. In both cases only the men are mentioned. But other scriptures reveal that Noah and his family are saved (Genesis 7:21-23), as well as Lot and his two daughters (Genesis 19:29, 30). One thing is clear from this reference, and that is that in both Noah's and Lot's day, only one group remains alive — the other group is "taken" or destroyed. In Genesis 7:23 it says, "And every living substance was destroyed which was upon the face of the ground, both man, and cattle, and the creeping things, and the fowl of the heaven; and they were destroyed from the earth: and Noah only remained alive, and they that were with him in the ark."

In their theory, those that believe in the rapture have one group going to heaven secretly, while the other remains on earth to suffer the supposed tribulation. But when the disciples asked, "Where, Lord?" after hearing the thrice repeated "one taken and the other left (Luke 17:34-37), Jesus said, "Wheresoever the body is, thither will the eagles be gathered together" (verse 37). This illustration is not one of bliss in glory. It is a plain description of death. The people are reported as being in "bed," "grinding," or "in the field." The grammatical structure suggests that the question is not concerning where they are, for that is revealed in the context. Rather, it refers to where they are "taken" or going. In other words, in consistency with the preceding analogies they are "taken" to death or destruction just as in Noah's or Lot's day. This illustration of eagles is found in the book of Job. "Doth the eagle mount up at thy command, and make her nest on high? She dwelleth and abideth on the rock, upon the crag of the rock, and the strong place. From thence she seeketh the prey, and her eyes behold afar off. Her young ones also suck up blood: and where the slain are, there is she" (Job 39:27-30). The idea of the wicked being taken first is in harmony with the parable of the wheat and the tares. The angels come and sever the tares, bind them to be burned, and then gather the wheat (Matthew 13:24-30, 37-43).

The problem is that most Christians use the word "taken" as a positive action. The truth is that this word has positive and negative outcomes depending on the context. It is said of Jesus, "Then the soldiers of the governor took Jesus into the common hall, and gathered unto him the whole band of soldiers" (Matthew 27:27). It is here that they place a "crown of thorns," "mock him," and "spit upon him." Then they led him to be crucified (Matthew 27:27-31). Notice that the word "took" is the same Greek word (*paralambano*) translated in Matthew as "taken."

Since Jesus promised to return and "receive" unto himself (John 14:3) the saved, it is understandable why Christians assume that this is when they are taken. The reality is that both Matthew 24 and Luke 17 are not addressing the destiny of the saved, but rather the fate of the ill prepared. The destiny of the righteous is spoken of in John 14:1-3, 1 Corinthians 15, and 1 Thessalonians 4:13-17: the wicked's fate is found in Revelation 6:14-17 and Revelation 19:11-21. The point is that Jesus is speaking to believers. He is using what happened before as a warning to them and future generations that they do not become like the antediluvians and lose their way. They must watch!

Luke 23:43
And Jesus said unto him, Verily I say unto thee,
To day shalt thou be with me in paradise.

Answer
Many take this text to prove that people go immediately to heaven when they die. However, Jesus could not have been making such a promise, for He himself said to Mary three days later on Sunday morning, "Touch me not; for I am not

yet ascended to my Father: but go to my brethren, and say unto them, I ascend unto my Father, and your Father; and to my God, and your God" (John 20:17). Jesus died on Friday, but the thieves did not. They had their legs broken because they were still alive. So Christ and the thieves did not even die on the same day. (See John 19:31-33). Where then lies the problem? In the Greek language there are no punctuation marks. Hence in the translation from Greek into English the comma was placed before the word "today" rather than after. Here is an example as to how a comma can change the meaning of a sentence. "A woman without her man is nothing!" Now let's add some commas. "A woman, without her, man is nothing!" The added commas change the meaning completely. Thus the assurance was, "I am telling you today, you will be with me in paradise." The converted convict was asking to be remembered when Christ went into His kingdom. Jesus taught His believers to pray, "Thy kingdom come." So, when His kingdom comes in the future, the thief will have his plea realized. As Jesus well said, "And this is the Father's will which hath sent me, that of all which he hath given me I should lose nothing, but should raise it up again at the last day. And this is the will of him that sent me, that every one which seeth the Son, and believeth on him, may have everlasting life: and I will raise him up at the last day" (John 6:39, 40).

John 1:17

*For the law was given by Moses, but grace
and truth came by Jesus Christ.*

Answer

It was Moses that gave the law to Israel. Moses was given that law by God. (See Deuteronomy 4:13.) What is the meaning of this verse? John is making a comparison between what Moses did and what Christ did. He was not dealing with time, but rather continues to magnify Christ's person above all others. It is like the sun that outshines the brightness of the moon. In other words, Moses, who was highly regarded as giving the law, does not compare to Jesus, who gave us grace and truth. But when did Christ give this grace and truth? Grace and truth did not originate when Jesus appeared as a man on earth. Grace was around in Noah's day (Genesis 6:8). Truth was present in the days of Abraham (Genesis 24:27). Israel found grace in the wilderness (Jeremiah 31:2). And Paul writes, "Who hath saved us, and called us with an holy calling, not according to our works, but according to his own purpose and grace, which was given us in Christ Jesus before the world began" (2 Timothy 1:9). What John is saying is that Christ is the originator of grace and truth. Jesus Himself claims, "I am the way, the truth, and the life" (John 14:6).

John 2:3-6

And when they wanted wine, the mother of Jesus saith unto him, They have no wine. Jesus saith unto her, Woman, what have I to do with thee? mine hour is not yet come. His mother saith unto the servants, Whatsoever he saith unto you, do it. And there were set there six waterpots of stone, after the manner of the purifying of the Jews, containing two or three firkins apiece.

Answer

The Bible warns, "Wine is a mocker, strong drink is raging: and whosoever is deceived thereby is not wise" (Proverbs 20:1). In chapter 23 it says, "Who hath woe? who hath sorrow? who hath contentions? who hath babbling? who hath wounds without cause? who hath redness of eyes? They that tarry long at the wine; they that go to seek mixed wine. Look not thou upon the wine when it is red, when it giveth his colour in the cup, when it moveth itself aright. At the last it biteth like a serpent, and stingeth like an adder" (Proverbs 23:29-32). Yet there are those that insist that Christ in this miracle made fermented wine. The dilemma is in the translation of the word. The Bible translators interpret the same Hebrew word in English as either "wine" or "new wine." Christ the Creator, and who through the Holy Spirit inspired these two statements, could not have contradicted His counsel. Jesus made "good wine," or "new wine."

Here is how the Bible refers to this "new wine." "For how great is his goodness, and how great is his beauty! corn shall make the young men cheerful, and new wine the maids" (Zechariah 9:17). "So shall thy barns be filled with plenty, and thy presses shall burst out with new wine" (Proverbs 3:10). "Thus saith the LORD, As the new wine is found in the cluster, and one saith, Destroy it not; for a blessing is in it: so will I do for my servants' sakes, that I may not destroy them all" (Isaiah 65:8). From these three references it is clear that new wine is grape juice. It makes people "cheerful" and there is a "blessing in it." Christ Himself did not imbibe. His example is clear. When on the cross, if there was ever a time when drinking fermented wine would have been excusable, it would have been then. In His torturous pain "they gave him vinegar to drink mingled with gall: and when he had tasted thereof, he would not drink" (Matthew 27:34). The same is recorded in Mark 15:23: "And they gave him to drink wine mingled with myrrh: but he received it not."

It is the new wine that Jesus promised He would not drink again until He drank it in the kingdom. "And he took the cup, and gave thanks, and gave it to them, saying, Drink ye all of it; For this is my blood of the new testament, which is shed for many for the remission of sins. But I say unto you, I will not drink henceforth of this fruit of the vine, until that day when I drink it new with you in my Father's kingdom" (Matthew 26:27-29). In the kingdom there will be no fermentation, for nothing will decay. Therefore, Jesus made new wine.

John 3:13

And no man hath ascended up to heaven, but he that came down from heaven, even the Son of man which is in heaven.

Answer

The subject at hand in John chapter 3 is conversion, the mysterious working of the Holy Spirit in this process, and the role that Jesus plays in man's salvation. When in exasperation Nicodemus retorted, "How can these things be?" (verse 9), Jesus said, "Art thou a master of Israel, and knowest not these things?" (verse 10). Jesus said, "If I have told you earthly things, and ye believe not, how shall ye believe, if I tell you of heavenly things?" (verse 12). Since these truths were divine, it necessitated a divine being to explain them. Jesus was that person! He is the one that originated in heaven. Before Jesus had incarnated, there were three humans who originated from the earth and had gone to heaven. These three are Enoch, Elijah (Genesis 5:24; 2 Kings 2:11), and Moses. Elijah and Moses are the ones recorded as visiting the Savior, and were seen by the disciples (Matthew 17:3). Luke records the following: "And as he prayed, the fashion of his countenance was altered, and his raiment was white and glistering. And, behold, there talked with him two men, which were Moses and Elias: Who appeared in glory, and spake of his decease which he should accomplish at Jerusalem" (Luke 9:29-31).

Take note that this is the only time in all of Holy Writ that mention is made of this phenomenon. Also notice that nothing is mentioned about them coming back and giving a report on heaven. Jesus knew about these three. Why did He make the statement? He is making it clear that salvation only comes through Him! (See verses 14-21.) In John chapter six Christ said, "For the bread of God is he which cometh down from heaven, and giveth life unto the world. For I came down from heaven, not to do mine own will, but the will of him that sent me. And this is the Father's will which hath sent me, that of all which he hath given me I should lose nothing, but should raise it up again at the last day. And this is the will of him that sent me, that every one which seeth the Son, and believeth on him, may have everlasting life: and I will raise him up at the last day" (verses 33, 38-40). Peter exclaims the same truth. He says, "Neither is there salvation in any other: for there is none other name under heaven given among men, whereby we must be saved" (Acts 4:12). Since no one else can save; Jesus is the only one who can. He is the only one who originated in heaven, and thus can be the only one to accurately give a correct explanation of heavenly things and salvation.

John 5:24

Verily, verily, I say unto you, He that heareth my word, and believeth on him that sent me, hath everlasting life, and shall not come into condemnation; but is passed from death unto life.

Answer

This verse of scripture can be misconstrued as meaning that a person who believes in Christ will not die. This interpretation is incorrect, and the Scriptures can show its error. John the Baptist, the greatest prophet that ever lived, was beheaded (Matthew 14:10-12). Lazarus believed in Christ and died (John 11: 1-35). Peter, Christ's disciple, was told that he would die (John 21:18, 19). James, John's brother, was killed by Herod (Acts 12:1, 2). Though death would eventually come to all His disciples, Jesus promised He would return to the earth to take them to where He is (John 14:1-3). The words, "shall not come into condemnation" simply mean that once a person is forgiven, he stands pardoned. As Jesus said to the woman caught in adultery, "neither do I condemn thee: Go, and sin no more" (John 8:11).

The phrases "hath everlasting life" and "passed from death to life" refer to a wonderful truth. When a person accepts Christ as Lord and Savior they begin the process of everlasting life. Jesus said, "Whoso eateth my flesh, and drinketh my blood, hath eternal life; and I will raise him up at the last day" (John 6:54). Notice that by eating and drinking the emblems of the Lord's Supper, one has eternal life. However, they, though they die, must be raised in the "last day." And in 1 John 5:11, 12, it says, "And this is the record, that God hath given to us eternal life, and this life is in his Son. He that hath the Son hath life; and he that hath not the Son of God hath not life." Eternal life begins for the believer that accepts into his heart the Life-giver. As a sinner he is condemned to death (Romans 6:23), but by accepting the Savior he passes into the hope of eternal life.

John 7:39

But this spake he of the Spirit, which they that believe on him should receive: for the Holy Ghost was not yet given; because that Jesus was not yet glorified.

Answer

This statement of John is in reference to the gift of the Holy

Ghost that had been promised in the day of Pentecost (Acts 1:4-5, 8). The Spirit of God was already present before this point in time. He came upon Mary (Matthew 1:18, 20), John the Baptist (Luke 1:15), and Jesus (Matthew 3:16). That the Holy Spirit was active before this time is evident in the Old Testament as well. He was present in the days of Noah (Genesis 6:3). In reference to Joseph, Pharaoh said unto his servants, "Can we find such a one as this is, a man in whom the Spirit of God is?" (Genesis 41:38). In the wilderness, God gave His Spirit to the elders of Israel. "And the LORD came down in a cloud, and spake unto him, and took of the spirit that was upon him, and gave it unto the seventy elders: and it came to pass, that, when the spirit rested upon them, they prophesied, and did not cease" (Numbers 11:25). Joshua was full of the Spirit (Deuteronomy 34:9). The book of Judges is replete with people filled with the Spirit (chapters 3-15). Ezekiel was a recipient of the Spirit (Ezekiel 11:5). In fact, the Old Testament prophets could have never written the Bible without the Spirit inspiring them on what to write (2 Peter 1:20, 21).

John 8:51

Verily, verily, I say unto you,
If a man keep my saying, he shall never see death.

Answer

This is obviously referring to the second death. Even the apostles experienced the first death. (See my comments on John 5:24.) "Elisha died, and they buried him" (2 Kings 13:20). This was the man filled with a double portion of the Spirit. As the scriptures say, "And as it is appointed unto men once to die" (Hebrews 9:27). John the revelator writes, "Blessed and holy is he that hath part in the first resurrection: on such the second death hath no power" (Revelation 20:6).

The first death is not a punishment as many people believe. It affects the righteous as well as the wicked. It is the second death from which Christ came to deliver His people. Jesus promised, "He that hath an ear, let him hear what the Spirit saith unto the churches; He that overcometh shall not be hurt of the second death" (Revelation 2:11). This is the death that in contrast to eternal life Jesus is referring to when He said, "For God so loved the world, that he gave his only begotten Son, that whosoever believeth in him should not perish, but have everlasting life" (John 3:16). In the same contrasting language Paul wrote, "For the wages of sin is death; but the gift of God is eternal life through Jesus Christ our Lord" (Romans 6:23).

John 9:31

Now we know that God heareth not sinners: but if any man be a worshipper of God, and doeth his will, him he heareth.

Answer

This statement was made by the young man who had been healed of blindness in defense of Christ. The term "sinner" was in reference to an evil person versus a good person. It is not to be taken in regards to hearing the prayers of sinners. The promise is, "If we confess our sins, he is faithful and just to forgive us our sins, and to cleanse us from all unrighteousness" (1 John 1:9). Obviously, it is a sinner that confesses sins, and God promises to forgive. God promises, "If my people, which are called by my name, shall humble themselves, and pray, and seek my face, and turn from their wicked ways; then will I hear from heaven, and will forgive their sins, and will heal their land" (2 Chronicles 7: 14).

John 10:27-29

My sheep hear my voice, and I know them, and they follow

me: And I give unto them eternal life; and they shall never perish, neither shall any man pluck them out of my hand. My Father, which gave them me, is greater than all; and no man is able to pluck them out of my Father's hand.

Answer

As stated before in my comments on John 5:24, eternal life begins when a person connects himself with Christ, the source of life. But it is the second part of this text that needs addressing. Many take these verses to prove the "once saved, always saved" teaching. But looking closely at this text, one can quickly see that the emphasis is on "neither shall any man" or "no man" be able to pull them out of God's hand. In other words, no other person can yank you out; not even the devil. This does not mean, however, that you personally cannot. That a person is locked into salvation is true as long as the choice on the part of the believer is exercised to stay attached. However, God made man and angels free moral agents. This means that the will must be engaged. God does not save man against his own will. This truth is revealed throughout the Scriptures.

In the Old Testament we have the story of King Saul, the first king of Israel. He was converted and given the Spirit. We read concerning him, "And it was so, that when he had turned his back to go from Samuel, God gave him another heart: and all those signs came to pass that day. And when they came thither to the hill, behold, a company of prophets met him; and the Spirit of God came upon him, and he prophesied among them" (1 Samuel 10:9, 10). Sadly, though, because of his rebellion (1 Samuel 15:23), "the Spirit of the LORD departed from Saul" (1 Samuel 16:14). He ended up a lost man. The record states, "So Saul died for his transgression which he committed against the LORD, even against the word of the LORD, which he kept not, and also for asking counsel of one that had a familiar spirit, to enquire of it" (1 Chronicles 10:13). In Ezekiel the Lord said, "The righteousness of the righteous shall not deliver him in the day of his transgression." Nor will the wicked die if he repents and turns from his sins. (See Ezekiel 33:12-19). In the New Testament the same truth is taught. Paul wrote, "Thou wilt say then, The branches were broken off, that I might be grafted in. Well; because of unbelief they were broken off, and thou standest by faith. Be not highminded, but fear: For if God spared not the natural branches, take heed lest he also spare not thee. Behold therefore the goodness and severity of God: on them which fell, severity; but toward thee, goodness, if thou continue in his goodness: otherwise thou also shalt be cut off " (Romans 11:19-22). To the Hebrews he warned, "But Christ as a son over his own house; whose house are we, if we hold fast the confidence and the rejoicing of the hope firm unto the end. Take heed, brethren, lest there be in any of you an evil heart of unbelief, in departing from the living God" (Hebrews 3:6, 12). Note that the condition is "if we hold fast." Then he says, "For it is impossible for those who were once enlightened, and have tasted of the heavenly gift, and were made partakers of the Holy Ghost, And have tasted the good word of God, and the powers of the world to come, If they shall fall away, to renew them again unto repentance; seeing they crucify to themselves the Son of God afresh, and put him to an open shame" (Hebrews 6:4-6).

Notice that it is possible for a person that has been a partaker of the Holy Ghost, "by which ye are sealed" (Ephesians 4:30), to "fall away." Peter says, "For if after they have escaped the pollutions of the world through the knowledge of the Lord and Saviour Jesus Christ, they are again entangled therein, and overcome, the latter end is worse with them than the beginning. For it had been better for them not to have known the way of righteousness, than, after they have known it, to turn from the holy commandment delivered unto them" (2 Peter 2:20, 21). Even angels who were once with God chose to no longer be with Him (Jude 6). God will hold on to you as long as you choose not to separate from Him. "Ye therefore, beloved, seeing ye know these things before, beware lest ye also, being led away with the error of the wicked, fall from your own stedfastness" (2 Peter 3:17).

John 11:26

And whosoever liveth and believeth
in me shall never die. Believest thou this?

Answer

Jesus is speaking to Martha, who is grieving over the death of her brother Lazarus. Obviously, Jesus is not negating the faith and belief on the part of Lazarus, who was considered to be "Him whom thou loveth" (John 11:3) by Him. Jesus had just talked to her about the resurrection (verse 25). And the focus is on the reality that "he that believeth in me, though he were dead, yet shall he live." Christ was giving the assurance of victory over the grave in as much as He is the "resurrection and the life." Consequently, if a believer were to die, through Christ he would live again and never die the second death. Jesus promised, "He that overcometh shall not be hurt of the second death" (Revelation 2:11).

John 12:25

He that loveth his life shall lose it; and he that hateth his life
in this world shall keep it unto life eternal.

Answer

Here the Lord is using language that can be easily

misunderstood. The Greek word for hate is *miseo*. The meaning needs to be determined by its use in the context. In Luke 14:26 Jesus said, "If any man come to me, and hate not his father, and mother, and wife, and children, and brethren, and sisters, yea, and his own life also, he cannot be my disciple." Yet in another place he said, "Love ye your enemies" (Luke 6:35).

It would be very unlikely as well as contradictory for Christ to encourage hate for loved ones and love for enemies. So what is the meaning? The answer can be understood from the perspective of the Ten Commandments. "Thou shalt love the Lord thy God with all thy heart, and with all thy soul, and with all thy mind. This is the first and great commandment. And the second is like unto it, Thou shalt love thy neighbor as thyself" (Matthew 22:37-39). We are encouraged to love God above all others. God, the One who gave us our parents, should have the first place in our lives.

The word "hate" in this usage makes it clear that this is not "hate" in the usual sense of the word. In the Bible, "to hate" oftentimes should be understood to simply mean to "love less." For example in Deuteronomy 21:15–17 it says, "If a man have two wives, one beloved and another hated, and they have born him children, both the beloved and the hated; and if the firstborn son be hers that was hated: Then it shall be, when he maketh his sons to inherit that which he hath, that he may not make the son of the beloved firstborn before the son of the hated, which is indeed the firstborn: But he shall acknowledge the son of the hated for the firstborn, by giving him a double portion of all that he hath: for he is the beginning of his strength; the right of the firstborn in his."

This was the case with Jacob and his two wives, Rachel and

Leah. "And he went in also unto Rachel, and he loved also Rachel more than Leah, and served with him yet seven other years. And when the LORD saw that Leah was hated, he opened her womb: but Rachel was barren" (Genesis 29:30, 31). It is not unlikely that in such case the husband's affection for the children of the favored wife would be very much more marked. Jacob's relationship with Leah proves that he did not "hate" her in the sense that the word generally conveys. He simply felt and showed less affection for her than he did for her sister.

This is the same way that Jesus spoke of having two masters. He said, "No man can love two masters: for either he will hate the one, and love the other; or else he will hold to the one, and despise the other" (Matthew 6:24). What he is saying is that it is not possible to love two exactly alike. One will be loved more, and the other less. The word "hates" indicates nothing more than a less intense degree of love. To love life as supreme above the love for God is to love Him less. But to "hate" (love less) life and love God more is life.

John 20:23
Whose soever sins ye remit, they are remitted unto them; and whose soever sins ye retain, they are retained.

Answer
This is the only text in all of the Scriptures like it. Therefore, to understand its meaning, we must find out from the rest of the New Testament how the apostles of Christ understood its appropriate application. What is interesting about this passage of Scriptures is that there is an absence in all of Luke, Peter, James, Jude, John, or Paul's writings exercising the supposed inherent power given to the disciples to forgive sins. The only applications dealing with the remission of

sin are found in Acts 2:38 where it says, "Then Peter said unto them, Repent, and be baptized every one of you in the name of Jesus Christ for the remission of sins, and ye shall receive the gift of the Holy Ghost." Also in Acts 10:43, where Peter said, "To him give all the prophets witness, that through his name whosoever believeth in him shall receive remission of sins." Notice that though some claim Peter to be the first pope, he does not say that he can forgive sins, but rather that forgiveness can be found solely in Christ.

When Christ was being charged with speaking blasphemes (see John 10:32, 33) because he claimed to have the power to forgive sins he did not retract nor deny it. Why not? Because Jesus, being God (see John 1:1-3), had the "power on earth to forgive sins" (Matthew 9:6).

Never is there found any evidence in the book of Acts (that show the results of the believers receiving the Holy Spirit) of the apostles forgiving sin. Paul writes, "Whom God hath set forth to be a propitiation through faith in his blood, to declare his righteousness for the remission of sins that are past, through the forbearance of God" (Romans 3:25). That they believed that sins could be remitted is true, but not that they had power to do so, but rather that God could do it. Paul states in Act 22:16, "And now why tarriest thou? arise, and be baptized, and wash away thy sins, calling on the name of the Lord." Otherwise, all mention of sins being removed in the New Testament is by virtue of the Lord remitting them. John wrote, "If we confess our sins, he is faithful and just to forgive us our sins, and to cleanse us from all unrighteousness" (1 John 1:9).

No doubt that in the text in question Jesus is reiterating the counsel He had before stated in Matthew 18:1-15,

21-35 concerning the responsibility he placed upon them as church leaders to care for the spiritual needs of the individual member, and the authority of the church. But the personal power to forgive sins they understood not to be in themselves, but in whom they pointed to. "Be it known unto you therefore, men and brethren, that through this man is preached unto you the forgiveness of sins: And by him all that believe are justified from all things, from which ye could not be justified by the law of Moses" (Acts 13:38, 39).

Acts 10:13
And there came a voice to him, Rise, Peter; kill, and eat.

Answer

God gave the apostle Peter this vision in correlation with Cornelius the centurion's vision. (See Acts 10:1-8.) The disciples needed to get beyond the Jewish barriers of prejudice against other groups of people. The gospel needed to be preached to the Gentiles, but it was not being done. The dream of Peter shook him up. He had spent three and one-half years with Christ, and at least another year had gone by after the great day of Pentecost; yet Peter had never been told to eat unclean foods. He said, "Not so, Lord; for I have never eaten any thing that is common or unclean" (Acts 10:14). This vision included "all manner of fourfooted beasts of the earth, and wild beasts, and creeping things, and fowls of the air" (verse 12).

It is interesting that people who use this text usually try to justify eating pork or shellfish. Others say that Christ cleansed all food, yet Peter was not aware of any such practice or counsel from his Lord. At the onset, Peter did not understand the vision. It says, "While Peter doubted in himself what this vision which he had seen should mean" (verse 17). While he was bewildered, the Holy Ghost commanded him to go with the strangers that had been sent by Cornelius. (See verse 19.) Upon his arrival he finds a crowd of Gentiles waiting for him, and that is when he gets the message. He says, "Ye know how that it is an unlawful thing for a man that is a Jew to keep company, or come unto one of another nation; but God hath shewed me that I should not call any man common or unclean" (verse 28). Peter does not need people today to give a different slant than that which he plainly lays out.

It was not animals that God was dealing with; he was not cleansing animals, but rather people from their sins. "God has shown me today!" The barriers of exclusivism were finally broken down, and now the apostles turned their efforts to reaching all, Greeks, Gentiles, and Jews.

The Bible is consistent. This demarcation between the clean and unclean animal continues even until the day that the Lord returns. Isaiah writes concerning the day of the Lord: "For, behold, the LORD will come with fire, and with his chariots like a whirlwind, to render his anger with fury, and his rebuke with flames of fire. For by fire and by his sword will the LORD plead with all flesh: and the slain of the LORD shall be many. They that sanctify themselves, and purify themselves in the gardens behind one tree in the midst, eating swine's flesh, and the abomination, and the mouse, shall be consumed together, saith the LORD" (Isaiah 66:15-17).

Acts 12:15

And they said unto her, Thou art mad. But she constantly affirmed that it was even so. Then said they, It is his angel.

Answer

The damsel Rhoda heard knocking at the door. When she

went to enquire as to whom it was, she immediately knew. "And when she knew Peter's voice, she opened not the gate for gladness, but ran in, and told how Peter stood before the gate." They could not believe that it could possibly be Peter. They knew by experience that an angel had delivered them before. This took place earlier when the leaders "laid their hands on the apostles, and put them in the common prison. But the angel of the Lord by night opened the prison doors, and brought them forth, and said, Go, stand and speak in the temple to the people all the words of this life" (Acts 5:18-20). The disciples were incredulous. And now since there was no possible way that it could be Peter, they erroneously concluded that Peter's guardian angel was at work again. The same thing happened when Jesus appeared to them after the resurrection. They "were terrified and affrighted, and supposed that they had seen a spirit" (Luke 24:37). Apparently, though the Master had taught them by precept and example that people resurrected from the dead, they still clung to their superstition of spirits. It had happened before when Jesus walked on the water. "But when they saw him walking upon the sea, they supposed it had been a spirit, and cried out: For they all saw him, and were troubled" (Mark 6:49, 50). Once more their skeptical spirit leads them to make a wrong assertion.

There are those that take this text and teach that humans become angels when they die. That supposition is unwarranted. Angels are a different order of creation (Psalm 8:5; Hebrews 2:16). They existed before man (Job 38:4-7). They were in the Garden of Eden before the death of Abel, the first human fatality (Genesis 3:24). Children have guardian angels (Matthew 18:10) while they are still alive. In the resurrection, man will "be as the angels" (Matthew 22:30), not angels! The angels come to "gather his elect" at the second coming (Mark 13:27).

Acts 15:19, 20

Wherefore my sentence is, that we trouble not them,
which from among the Gentiles are turned
to God: But that we write unto them,
that they abstain from pollutions of idols, and from
fornication, and from things strangled and from blood.

Answer

The apostles were challenged by the attempted reintroduction of circumcision and other Jewish ceremonies into the new Christian faith. (See verse 1 and 5.) The phrase "the Law of Moses" is found 22 times in the entire Bible. It refers to that which was contained in the book of the Law of Moses, not the Ten Commandment law. Because of the problems created by the believing Pharisees, it was necessary to bring the issues before the leadership of the church in Jerusalem. When the questions were discussed, James, after listening to the details, gave his sentence. This meeting was not to discuss all that the Bible teaches or that the Gentiles were expected to follow, for verse 21 says, "For Moses of old time hath in every city them that preach him, being read in the Synagogues every Sabbath day." In other words, they are able to learn every Sabbath all the rest of what the Bible teaches. The controversy was over the matters mentioned.

To say, or to suggest, that all that was required of the Gentiles in order to be Christian was to abstain from the four things mentioned is incorrect and an exaggeration of the Scriptures. They were not at liberty to steal, kill, bear false witness, commit adultery, covet, or be in violation of any of God's commandments (see Romans 13:8-11). Therefore, what was discussed and recorded are the issues at hand. To the Galatians and Ephesians, Paul (the one presenting the case on behalf of the Gentiles) wrote counsel addressing the appropriate behavior and attitude that the Gentiles were to follow. (See Galatians 5:16-26; Ephesians 4:27-32.) You will note that different issues arose in Corinth. Paul addressed those matters not as the sum and total of what the Corinthian believers were to follow, but rather dealt with the particular beliefs or practices they needed to correct.

Romans 4:17

(As it is written, I have made thee a father of many nations,) before him whom he believed, even God, who quickeneth the dead, and calleth those things which be not as though they were.

Answer

Some people think that this text refers to stimulating dead people—that is not what it means. The term "quickens" means to make alive. Jesus said, "For as the Father raiseth up the dead, and quickeneth them; even so the Son quickeneth whom he will" (John 5:12). It is "God, who quickeneth all things" (1 Timothy 6:13), or makes, or gives life. Paul is specifically referring here to the promise God made to Abraham concerning the miraculous birth of Isaac (verses 18-21). This also includes the power God has to call back to life those who are dead. The Lord says, "Thy dead men shall live, together with my dead body shall they arise. Awake and sing, ye that dwell in dust: for thy dew is as the dew of herbs, and the earth shall cast out the dead" (Isaiah 26:19). And in John 11:25 He said, "I am the resurrection, and the life: he that believeth in me, though he were dead, yet shall he live." Paul is making reference to the One who has power to call into being something from nothing. The greatest example is the creation of the earth and all that it contains. (See Genesis chapter 1 and 2.) It also includes

His power to forecast the future. God declares, "I am God, and there is none like me, Declaring the end from the beginning, and from ancient times the things that are not yet done, saying, My counsel shall stand, and I will do all my pleasure" (Isaiah 46:9, 10).

Romans 5:13

For until the law sin was in the world:
but sin is not imputed when there is no law.

Answer

The biblical definition of sin is: "Whosoever committeth sin transgresseth also the law: for sin is the transgression of the law" (1 John 3:4). Therefore, in order for Adam and Eve to have sinned, there had to be a law. A quick look at the first recorded temptation in Genesis chapter 3 reveals that Eve violated:

1. The first commandment. She accepted the deception and thus desired to be like God (verse 5).

2. The fifth commandment. She did not honor her Father (verses 2 and 3).

3. The sixth commandment. She was told that she would die (verse 3).

4. The eighth commandment. She stole — took that which did not belong to her (verse 6).

5. The tenth commandment. She saw and "desired" (verse 6).

Paul is simply stating that before the law was written there was sin in the world. At least 400 years before Sinai, Abraham kept the law, for God said, "Because that Abraham obeyed my voice, and kept my charge, my commandments, my statutes, and my laws" (Genesis 26:5). There is no question that the law existed before Sinai. Here are some examples: The Sabbath existed in Eden (Genesis 2:2, 3). Cain killed Abel, and God called that sin (Genesis 4:6-8). Stealing was punished (Genesis 31:32). Jacob knew that it was wrong to have false gods (Genesis 35:1-5). Joseph, likewise, knew that adultery was wrong when he said, "How then can I do this great wickedness, and sin against God?" (Genesis 39:9). It was wrong to lie (Genesis 26:9-11). In fact, all of the Ten Commandments can be traced through the book of Genesis and Exodus before they were written in Sinai.

Romans 7:4

Wherefore, my brethren, ye also are become dead to the law by the body of Christ; that ye should be married to another, even to him who is raised from the dead, that we should bring forth fruit unto God.

Answer

According to the Bible, death is the release from the marital contract (Romans 7:1-3; Deuteronomy 25:5, 6). Paul is using this fact to teach that a person in sin is bonded to the devil. "Know ye not, that to whom ye yield yourselves servants to obey, his servants ye are to whom ye obey; whether of sin unto death, or of obedience unto righteousness?" (Romans 6:16). However, when a person is converted and baptized, he is considered to be dead to sin (Romans 6:3, 4). Then, "he that is dead is freed from sin" (verse 7). The transfer of allegiance is made in conversion. Paul affirms, "But God be thanked, that ye were the servants of sin, but ye have obeyed from the heart that form of doctrine which was delivered you. Being then made free from sin, ye became the servants of righteousness" (Romans 6:17-18). The force of Paul's words concerning Roman 7:4 is not that the law dies, but rather that the sinner dies to sin, and begins to live for and with Christ. Paul often used marital language to express the intimate relationship that should exist between Christ and the believer. He declares, "for I have espoused you to one husband, that I may present you as a chaste virgin to Christ" (2 Corinthians 11:2).

Romans 10:4

For Christ is the end of the law
for righteousness to every one that believeth.

Answer

In the King James Version the word "end" is used 307 times in 291 verses. The way the word is used will determine its meaning. For example, it can mean to terminate (Genesis 6:13), to complete a period of time (Genesis 8:3), the furthest or most extreme part or point (Genesis 23:9), final outcome (Acts 7:19), a purpose (2 Corinthians 2:9), the finality (1 Corinthians 15:24), and a goal (Romans 14:9). Some use this text to prove that Christ ended the law. Did Christ come to do away with His law or sin? The answer is obvious; He came to do away with sin. What did the apostle Paul mean by this statement? The word "end" is used in other verses in the Bible. A quick look at three verses of Scripture will help us understand the meaning of the word in its usage, and what Paul meant. "Remember them which have the rule over you, who have spoken unto you the word of God: whose faith follow, considering the end of their conversation" (Hebrews 13:7). "Behold, we count them happy which endure. Ye have heard of the patience of Job, and have seen the end of the Lord; that the Lord is very pitiful, and of tender mercy" (James 5:11). "Receiving the end of your faith, even the salvation of your souls" (1 Peter 1:9). If the word "end" in these texts meant to finish, then faith is ended, and Christ is also finished. It is evident from these verses that the word "end" means goal, purpose or outcome. In other words, the goal of the law is to lead to Christ. The law reveals the sinner's condition, which in turn leads him to Christ for righteousness. In Titus, Paul says, "Now the end of the commandment is charity out of a pure heart, and of a good conscience, and of faith unfeigned" (Titus 1:5). Here he says that the purpose of the commandment is love out of a pure heart.

Romans 11:26

And so all Israel shall be saved: as it is written,
There shall come out of Sion the Deliverer,
and shall turn away ungodliness from Jacob:

Answer

According to Paul's writings, he does not see literal Israel as a nation, but rather spiritual Israel as a people saved. In the second chapter of Romans he states, "For he is not a Jew, which is one outwardly; neither is that circumcision, which is outward in the flesh: But he is a Jew, which is one inwardly; and circumcision is that of the heart, in the spirit, and not in the letter; whose praise is not of men, but of God" (Romans 2:28, 29). And again, "For they are not all Israel, which are of Israel: Neither, because they are the seed of Abraham, are they all children: but, In Isaac shall thy seed be called. That is, they which are the children of the flesh, these are not the children of God: but the children of the promise are counted for the seed" (Romans 9:6-8). The final Israel that will be saved will be made up of converted people of all "nations, and kindreds, and people, and tongues" (Revelation 7:9). The name Israel (which means "God prevails") was given to Jacob (which means "deceiver," or "supplanter"), resulting from his wrestling with God (Genesis 32:28). And those who, like Jacob, overcome, shall be grafted into the stock (Romans 11:17) and become spiritual Jews.

Concerning this teaching, Paul writes in Galatians, "There is neither Jew nor Greek, there is neither bond nor free, there is neither male nor female: for ye are all one in Christ Jesus. And if ye be Christ's, then are ye Abraham's seed, and heirs according to the promise" (Galatians 3:28, 29). "Is he the God of the Jews only? Is he not also of the Gentiles? Yes, of the Gentiles also" (Romans 3:29). From these references one can quickly see that Israel will be comprised of "a great multitude, which no man could number, of all nations, and kindreds, and people, and tongues," [who shall stand] "before the throne, and before the Lamb, clothed with white robes, and palms in their hands; And cried with a loud voice, saying, Salvation to our God which sitteth upon the throne, and unto the Lamb" (Revelation 7:9, 10). The Lord was emphatic in this point when he told the Jewish leaders, "And I say unto you, that many shall come from the east and west, and shall sit down with Abraham, and Isaac, and Jacob, in the kingdom of heaven. But the children of the kingdom shall be cast out into outer darkness: there shall be weeping and gnashing of teeth" (Matthew 8:11, 12).

Romans 14:1-6

"Him that is weak in the faith receive ye, but not to doubtful disputations. For one believeth that he may eat all things: another, who is weak, eateth herbs. Let not him that eateth despise him that eateth not; and let not him which eateth not judge him that eateth: for God hath received him. Who art thou that judgest another man's servant? to his own master he standeth or falleth. Yea, he shall be holden up: for God is able to make him stand. One man esteemeth one day above another: another esteemeth every day alike. Let every man be fully persuaded in his own mind. He that regardeth the day,

regardeth it unto the Lord; and he that regardeth not the day, to the Lord he doth not regard it. He that eateth, eateth to the Lord, for he giveth God thanks; and he that eateth not, to the Lord he eateth not, and giveth God thanks."

Answer

A surface reading of this text appears to suggest that any person who eats vegetables is a weak person. However, if Paul were declaring this as truth it would be in contradiction to the testimony of Daniel the prophet, who chose to eat a vegetarian diet (see Daniel chapter 1), and the original God-given diet (see Genesis 1:29). In 1 Corinthians 8:1-13 we find clear evidence that Paul is dealing with issues facing new believers who were Gentiles. They considered the partaking of food offered to idols as participating in idolatry: practices in which they had formerly engaged. "Ye know that ye were Gentiles, carried away unto these dumb idols, even as ye were led" (1 Corinthians 12:2), Paul wrote.

The same problem that existed in Rome was prevalent in Corinth. To the Corinthians Paul wrote: "Now as touching things offered unto idols, we know that we all have knowledge … As concerning therefore the eating of those things that are offered in sacrifice unto idols, we know that an idol is nothing in the world, and that there is none other God but one. But to us there is but one God, the Father, of whom are all things, and we in him; and one Lord Jesus Christ, by whom are all things, and we by him. Howbeit there is not in every man that knowledge: for some with conscience of the idol unto this hour eat it as a thing offered unto an idol; and their conscience being weak is defiled. But meat commendeth us not to God: for neither, if we eat, are we the better; neither, if we eat not, are we the worse. But take heed lest by any means this liberty of yours become a stumblingblock to them that are weak. For if any man see thee which hast knowledge sit at meat in the idol's temple, shall not the conscience of him which is weak be emboldened to eat those things which are offered to idols; And through thy knowledge shall the weak brother perish, for whom Christ died? But when ye sin so against the brethren, and wound their weak conscience, ye sin against Christ. Wherefore, if meat make my brother to offend, I will eat no flesh while the world standeth, lest I make my brother to offend" (1 Corinthians 8:1-13).

Paul uses the same wording found in Romans chapter 14 when addressing the Corinthian believers. The word "weak" he uses to refer to someone who has a sensitive conscience (notice verse 7). In both cases, Paul is concerned about the critical spirit or the overly pliant will on the part of some believers and, on the other hand, a don't care attitude on the part of the others. The subject matter is food offered to idols, not clean meats versus unclean meats. Some believers ate it, seeing it only as food, while another group felt that by eating the food they would be lending to idolatrous practices. Paul tells the sensitive brethren indirectly that their concern is unfounded. In other words, the food was not unfit to eat because it was offered to idols. An orange was still an orange. Conversely, he gently scolds the other who apparently is not concerned about their "good being evil spoken of " and showing no concern as to how their actions affected others.

In Romans chapter 14 he also addresses the issue of the Jewish feast days. He wrote to the Galatians, "Ye observe days, and months, and times, and years. I am afraid of you, lest I have bestowed upon you labour in vain" (Galatians 4:10, 11). Paul no doubt is referring to the ceremonial feast days. Apparently there was some squabble as to which feast days were to be kept. In these verses the focal point of Paul is transparent. He is not addressing the issue of what kinds of food are good and which are bad. Nor is he speaking of the Sabbath day as some assert; rather, he is speaking of having a judgmental spirit on the part of those overly conscientious about doing the "right thing," or trying to save themselves by the works of the Jewish festivals. He was also giving a gentle rebuke to those with such a liberal spirit that it didn't matter who they offended as long as they were "clear in their own conscience." These issues had the potential of dividing the church, and Paul was trying to avert such a split.

Romans 14:5, 6

One man esteemeth one day above another: another esteemeth
every day alike. Let every man be fully persuaded
in his own mind. He that regardeth the day, regardeth
it unto the Lord; and he that regardeth not the day,
to the Lord he doth not regard it.

Answer

The book of Romans was written by Paul around A.D. 55 to A.D. 56 from "Corinth at the end of his stay there, recorded in Acts 20:3."[1] He wrote it in regards to those doctrines that were in "dispute with the Judaizing Christians, and which Paul now regarded as finally established."[2] Some assume that Paul is writing this to inform the Roman believers that they need not worry about which day to worship. However, when Paul wrote this, the Sabbath, which was the day of worship, was not in question. All through the book of Acts, the only day of worship was the Sabbath. Notice that it was on the Sabbath day when Paul went to church. "And Paul, as his manner was, went in unto them, and three sabbath days reasoned with them out of the scriptures" (Acts 17:2).

---

1   KJV Bible, Cambridge University Press, Bible Dictionary, p. 124
2   Ibid

He was not alone in this matter. "And on the sabbath we went out of the city by a river side, where prayer was wont to be made; and we sat down, and spake unto the women which resorted thither. And a certain woman named Lydia, a seller of purple, of the city of Thyatira, which worshipped God, heard us: whose heart the Lord opened, that she attended unto the things which were spoken of Paul" (Acts 16:13, 14). Throughout the book of Acts there is constant reference to the apostles habit of Sabbathkeeping (see Acts 1:12; 13:14, 27, 42; 15:21; 16:13; 17:2; 18:4). In Paul's letter to the Hebrews he wrote, "There remains, then, a Sabbath-rest for the people of God" (Hebrews 4:9 NIV).

It is interesting that Paul addresses all the issues that people in his day were having problems with, e.g. adultery, worshipping false gods, disobedience to parents, stealing, having a judgmental spirit, misuse of spiritual gifts, false teachings, etc. But there are no arguments or debates in regards to which day to worship on. This very fact underscores the reality that to the believers the Sabbath was never a question.

What was therefore in question was not that which was ironclad in the Scriptures, and part of the unchanging Ten Commandments (Psalm 111:7, 8; Matthew 5:17,18), but rather the ceremonial Sabbaths. These are found listed in Leviticus 23. The feast days were referred to as Sabbath days. "Speak unto the children of Israel, saying, In the seventh month, in the first day of the month, shall ye have a sabbath, a memorial of blowing of trumpets, an holy convocation" (Leviticus 23:24). The Day of Atonement, which fell on the tenth day of the seventh month, was to be kept as a Sabbath. "It shall be unto you a sabbath of rest, and ye shall afflict your souls" (verse 32). These were the days that the Judaizers were trying to introduce into Christianity that Paul was addressing. They were "shadows of thing to come" (Colossians 2:17). The same issues were present among the Galatians to which Paul wrote, "But now, after that ye have known God, or rather are known of God, how turn ye again to the weak and beggarly elements, whereunto ye desire again to be in bondage? Ye observe days, and months, and times, and years. I am afraid of you, lest I have bestowed upon you labour in vain" (Galatians 4:9-11).

These feast days are still having their inroads into some current Christian denominations. However, from Paul's perspective they no longer need to be observed (see my comments on Colossians 2:14-17). The greater fear (as far as Paul was concerned) was the division that these arguments were having in the Christian churches, which Paul sought to allay by discouraging a judgmental attitude (see Romans 14:10-13). The same thing is true today. Some Christians keep Easter, some Christmas, some both. There are others that keep other religious holidays. Then, there are those Christians that feel strongly that neither should be observed. It was to this kind of condition that Paul was speaking to.

Romans 14:14

I know, and am persuaded by the Lord Jesus, that there is nothing unclean of itself: but to him that esteemeth any thing to be unclean, to him it is unclean.

Answer

This chapter has fomented many a battle between Christians. Nevertheless, the problem has to do with the way that Paul expresses his thoughts. In verse 1 Paul makes a reference to those that are "weak." This inference is not in regards to strength. Daniel was a vegetarian (Daniel 1:12-17) and was in better health than his counterparts. The issue here is that brethren began to have a judgmental attitude toward others (verses 4, 10, and 13). However, this same problem existed not just in Rome; it was also present among the Corinthian believers. In Corinthians chapter 8, however, he is clearer about the issue at hand and how to deal with it. Notice that he uses the word "weak" here relating to a "weak conscience" (verse 7). The term "weak conscience" means a sensitive conscience.

The practice in those days was of idolaters taking the food offered to idols and eating it, and then selling what remained (verse 10). Christians, who saw it only as food, bought it and ate it. But there were some believers who felt that this was being an accomplice to idolatry. So, Paul counseled, "If any of them that believe not bid you to a feast, and ye be disposed to go; whatsoever is set before you, eat, asking no question for conscience sake. But if any man say unto you, This is offered in sacrifice unto idols, eat not for his sake that shewed it, and for conscience sake: for the earth is the Lord's, and the fulness thereof: Conscience, I say, not thine own, but of the other: for why is my liberty judged of another man's conscience?" (1 Corinthians 10:27-29). Notice that the issue is not concerning what the scriptures designate as "clean" or "unclean" (see Leviticus 11), but whether or not food offered to idols (which to some Christians) would be considered "unclean." The food offered by the pagans in Lystra was not biblically unclean (Acts 14:13).

The other issue was concerning holidays or religious festivals. Paul had written to the Colossian believers that the Jewish feast days were done away with (Colossians 2:14-17). In Galatians he wrote: "Ye observe days, and months, and times, and years. I am afraid of you, lest I have bestowed upon you labour in vain" (Galatians 4:10). Apparently there were those who were being encouraged by Judaizers to return back to keeping the Jewish feast days. (See Galatians 2:14.) This had nothing to do with the Sabbath in as much as Paul himself observed the Sabbath. (See Acts 13:14, 42; 16:13; 17:2.) The apostle Paul is seeking to give good advice concerning issues that could become divisive and thus destroy the faith of those who were either young in the faith, or just highly sensitive.

Romans 14:21

It is good neither to eat flesh, nor to drink wine, nor any thing whereby thy brother stumbleth, or is offended, or is made weak.

Answer

Again Paul is suggesting an attitude that should be taken by those who did not see the food offered to idols as unclean as others did (1 Corinthians 8:1, 10). He winds up his discussion on this issue by writing, "Wherefore, if meat make my brother to offend, I will eat no flesh while the world standeth, lest I make my brother to offend" (1 Corinthians 8:13). He in no way is suggesting that a Christian can eat or drink anything, for he wrote, "Know ye not that ye are the temple of God, and that the Spirit of God dwelleth in you? If any man defile the temple of God, him shall God destroy; for the temple of God is holy, which temple ye are" (1 Corinthians 3:16, 17).

1 Corinthians 5:4, 5

In the name of our Lord Jesus Christ, when ye are gathered together, and my spirit, with the power of our Lord Jesus Christ, To deliver such an one unto Satan for the destruction

of the flesh, that the spirit may be saved in
the day of the Lord Jesus.

Answer

This text no doubt has been a very bothersome verse to many. For there are those who have taken it with a sense of gleeful manipulative reprisal on those whom they suppose to have spiritual authority over.

From this passage it appears that Paul has a relationship with Satan, such as a mother who tells her child, "Wait until your father comes home." But the Scriptures make it plain that Christ is the one that has the "keys of hell [the grave] and of death" (Revelation 1:18). And it is God, not Satan that Paul declares, "For whom the Lord loveth he chasteneth, and scourges every son whom he receiveth" (Hebrew 12:6). Why then this language?

Paul is apparently taking this idea from the book of Psalms, chapter 109. In verse 6, in referring to the wicked, it says: "Set thou a wicked man over him: and let Satan stand at his right hand." In the book of Job, the Lord, in dealing with Satan's charges against Job, said, "Behold, all that he hath is in thy power; only upon himself put not forth thine hand. So Satan went forth from the presence of the LORD." "And the LORD said unto Satan, Behold, he is in thine hand; but save his life" (Job 1:12; 2:6). Notice that Job suffers from the affliction of Satan not as a dead person in hell, but rather while living. The destruction of the flesh is a phrase Paul uses in reference to the sensual or carnal nature (see Mark 14:38; John 1:13; Romans 8:5-9; 13:14; Galatians 5:15-24). The "spirit" he is using to refer to the spiritual nature (see Galatians 5:15-24).

In the text in question Paul sees himself as a spokesperson on behalf of the Lord. In the preceding chapters Paul uses language such as, "Unto the married I command, yet not I, but the Lord," "But to the rest speak I, not the Lord" (1 Corinthians 7:10, 12). Therefore, being the spiritual overseer of the church, he uses his position to make certain recommendations and mandates. It is from this vantage point that he speaks.

Here he is most definitely dealing with people, who by virtue of their aggravated sinful choices should be excommunicated. By so doing, they would be disconnected from the Lord, and thereby (in his thinking) subject to the uninhibited workings of Satan. In today's vernacular, some people say, "You're going to hell," or, "Go to hell." Obviously, no one can command another person to such a destiny. The language simply suggests the loathsome and repugnant condition of the perpetrator and his offense.

Concerning people who turn their backs to the Lord, Jesus said, "He that is not with me is against me: and he that gathereth not with me scattereth. When the unclean spirit is gone out of a man, he walketh through dry places, seeking rest; and finding none, he saith, I will return unto my house whence I came out. And when he cometh, he findeth it swept and garnished. Then goeth he, and taketh to him seven other spirits more wicked than himself; and they enter in, and dwell there: and the last state of that man is worse than the first" (Luke 11:23-27). As a result, the offender is able to experience and see the reality of the maliciousness of the devil.

This condition Paul again describes when he wrote, "Holding the faith, and a good conscience; which some having put away concerning faith have made shipwreck: of whom is Hymanaeus and Alexander; whom I have delivered unto Satan, that they may learn not to blaspheme" (1 Timothy 1:19,

20). By writing this to the believers, Paul is making it obvious that the persons under question are no longer to be considered on Christ's side, but rather on Satan's. Nevertheless, in his second letter to the Corinthians, he appeals to the church for a spirit of forgiveness to the offender (see 2 Corinthians 2:5-11).

1 Corinthians 11:13

Judge in yourselves: is it comely
that a woman pray unto God uncovered?

Answer

There are several different denominations that insist on women covering their heads based on this text. While it is true that people can become irreverent in the house of worship, they can be irreverent irrespective of the restrictions imposed on them. Paul is cautioning believers as to what is proper deportment in the house of God. But though he makes a lot of different points about the issue, he concludes with this point: "Doth not even nature itself teach you, that, if a man have long hair, it is a shame unto him? But if a woman have long hair, it is a glory to her: for her hair is given her for a covering" (verses 13 and 14). Notice that Paul says, "Her hair is given her for a covering." Apparently there must have been different ideas as to whether men or women should cover themselves when worshipping. He gives his advice in the matter but finally concludes, "But if any man seem to be contentious, we have no such custom, neither the churches of God" (verse 16). In other words, don't make an issue of it.

1 Corinthians 14:2

For he that speaketh in an unknown tongue speaketh not
unto men, but unto God: for no man understandeth him;
howbeit in the spirit he speaketh mysteries.

Answer

In the book of Acts, chapter 2, we find the fulfillment of Christ's promise of the Spirit. On that day in Jerusalem there were "devout men, out of every nation" (Acts 2:5). The disciples only spoke to "Galilaeans" (verse 7). Yet, they had been commissioned to preach the gospel in Jerusalem and to the "uttermost parts of the earth" (Acts 1:8). But how, since they were only monolinguals? God gave them precisely what they needed — the ability to speak languages and dialects. (See Acts 2:6-12.) By this means those visiting Jerusalem heard the gospel in their own language, wherein they "were born." (See verse 8.) Thus the mission impossible became the mission accomplished — the gospel was now communicated to multilinguals, which in returning home could share it in many different languages.

So, the gift of tongues is languages. Yet there are many who use the scripture in question to suggest there exists a language that only God understands. This phenomenon is called "speaking in tongues." Some refer to it as an "angelic language." However, a closer look at the verse does not suggest the existence of an unknown language. The word "unknown" is a supplied word by the translator. The actual definition of the word "tongue" (in the Greek, *glossa*) in *Strong's Lexicon* is either referring to the actual organ, or a language or dialect. James 1:26 and 1 Peter 3:10 use the same Greek word concerning the organ.

The biblical narratives about this phenomenon reveal several things about tongues.

1. It is a real human foreign language (Acts 2:6-12).

2. An unknown language is not supposed to be spoken to those present unless there is an interpreter (verse 5, 27). It must be understood (verses 9-11, 16-19).

3. If there is no interpreter, then the tongue speaker is to be silent (verse 28).

4. It is not to be used for self-edification (verse 4).

5. Prophesying is preferred above this gift (verse 6).

6. Not all believers receive the gift of tongues (1 Corinthians 12:29, 30). Jesus was filled with the Holy Ghost, and there is no record of Him having this gift.

7. Tongues will end (1 Corinthians 13:8). Therefore, it cannot be a heavenly language.

8. Paul is not calling what the Corinthians are exercising angelic. Otherwise, when tongues cease, then the angels would remain mute.

9. Tongues are for the purpose of witnessing to non-believers (verses 21-23; Acts 1:8).

10. The recipients of the gift of tongues are not automatons; they are able to control what they say (verse 31-33).

11. When Paul received the Holy Ghost there is no mention of him receiving the supernatural gift of tongues (Acts 9:17-18). However, he was a linguist; he could speak in many languages (verses 18 and 19).

The whole import of 1 Corinthians 14 is to make sure of the motives and reasons for using spiritual gifts. Paul was admonishing that the believers endeavor in the church to "let all things be done decently and in order" (verse 40).

1 Corinthians 15:29

Else what shall they do which are baptized for the dead, if the dead rise not at all? Why are they then baptized for the dead?

Answer

The scriptures are crystal clear concerning salvation by proxy. The Psalmist wrote, "None of them can by any means redeem his brother, nor give to God a ransom for him" (Psalm 49:7). Ezekiel's writings also support this. Quoting the Lord, he wrote, "Though these three men, Noah, Daniel, and Job, were in it, they should deliver but their own souls by their righteousness, saith the Lord GOD. Though these three men were in it, as I live, saith the Lord GOD, they shall deliver neither sons nor daughters; they only shall be delivered, but the land shall be desolate. Though Noah, Daniel, and Job, were in it, as I live, saith the Lord GOD, they shall deliver neither son nor daughter; they shall but deliver their own souls by their righteousness" (Ezekiel 14:14, 16, 20). God is emphatic concerning personal responsibility for one's own sins and salvation. Again in Ezekiel He says, "The soul that sinneth, it shall die. The son shall not bear the iniquity of the father, neither shall the father bear the iniquity of the son: the righteousness of the righteous shall be upon him, and the wickedness of the wicked shall be upon him." (See Ezekiel 18:20-24.)

There are conditions for baptism.

1. A person must repent (Acts 2:38).

2. Must believe with all his heart in the Lord (Acts 8:36, 37).

3. Must be born again (John 3:3, 5).

4. Must die to the old sinful ways and begin living a new life (Romans 6:2-6).

5. Must be their own personal belief (Mark 16:16).

6. Must be taught (Matthew 28:19, 20). Dead people cannot make choices or believe (Ecclesiastes 9:5, 6).

Paul's whole argument in chapter 15 is the imperative of the Resurrection. Without Christ being raised, there is no hope. He then raises the question about those asleep, or dead (verses 17 and 18). Later on in the chapter he raises the issue of baptism. What about those who were baptized? In other words, the reason for baptism is to commemorate the death, burial, and resurrection of Christ (Romans 6:2-8), and that those who believe and are "baptized shall be saved" (Mark 16:16). Paul well understood the prominent role that baptism had in man's salvation. Therefore, he argues, what about those who were baptized? Did they get baptized for naught?

The problem with the text in question is simply the word "for." In the Greek the word can also mean "in consideration, in view of, or concerning." Having this understanding of the problem, the text then makes perfect sense. With this in mind let's read the verse again. "Else what shall they do which are baptized for [that is, those that are] the dead, if the dead rise not at all? Why are they then baptized for [that is, those that are] the dead." In today's language we would say it this way: "What about those who were baptized and died? If there is no resurrection then why were they baptized?"

1 Corinthians 15:50

Now this I say, brethren, that flesh and blood
cannot inherit the kingdom of God;
neither doth corruption inherit incorruption.

Answer

Jesus promised to resurrect His followers at His coming in the "last day" (John 6:39, 40, 44, 54), and guaranteed His disciples of the certainty of His return to take them to be where He is (John14:1-3). Job believed he would be restored back to flesh after his demise. He said, "For I know that my redeemer liveth, and that he shall stand at the latter day upon the earth: And though after my skin worms destroy this body, yet in my flesh shall I see God: Whom I shall see for myself, and mine eyes shall behold, and not another; though my reins be consumed within me" (Job 19:25-27). Isaiah wrote: "For as the new heavens and the new earth, which I will make, shall remain before me, saith the LORD, so shall your seed and your name remain. And it shall come to pass, that from one new moon to another, and from one sabbath to another, shall all flesh come to worship before me, saith the LORD" (Isaiah 66:22-23). It is obvious from these texts that people are resurrected as real people. Lazarus came back from the dead a resurrected human being (John 11:1-30). He and the others mentioned in the Scriptures came back to life in the flesh. In fact, if God had not separated Adam and Eve from the tree of life, they would have lived as eternal sinners (Genesis 3:22-24). They would not have died, but rather lived as humans. But God cannot permit eternal sinners, so He allows "death to pass upon all men" (Romans 5:12).

What is the meaning of this text? Paul is using the term "flesh" to mean carnal nature. Paul wrote to the Romans, "Because the carnal mind is enmity against God: for it is not subject to the law of God, neither indeed can be. So then they that are in the flesh cannot please God. But ye are not in the flesh, but in the Spirit, if so be that the Spirit of God dwell in you. Now if any man have not the Spirit of Christ, he is none of his" (Romans 8:7-9). To the Galatians he put it this way: "Walk in the Spirit, and ye shall not fulfil the lust of the flesh. For the flesh lusteth against the Spirit, and the Spirit against the flesh: and these are contrary the one to the other: so that ye cannot do the things that ye would. But if ye be led of the Spirit, ye are not under the law. Now the works of the flesh are manifest, which are these; Adultery, fornication, uncleanness, lasciviousness, Idolatry, witchcraft, hatred, variance, emulations, wrath, strife, seditions, heresies, Envyings, murders, drunkenness, revellings, and such like: of the which I tell you before, as I have also told you in time past, that they which do such things shall not inherit the kingdom of God" (Galatians 5:16-21).

Yes, there have been millions that have loved the Lord, but have passed into slumber until the Life-giver awakens them to eternal bliss. They will be resurrected and changed from mortality to immortality. (See 1 Corinthians 15:51-55.) They will once more be permitted to eat of the tree of life (Revelation 2:7; 22:14) and live forever.

2 Corinthians 3:7, 8

But if the ministration of death, written and engraven in stones, was glorious, so that the children of Israel could not stedfastly behold the face of Moses for the glory of his countenance; which glory was to be done away: 8 How shall not the ministration of the spirit be rather glorious?

Answer

The issue with this scriptural text has to do with the outshining of the "ministration of the spirit" versus the glory of the "ministration of death." The "glory" is done away with by the eclipsing light shed upon the soul through the means of the Holy Spirit. In this sense is the "ministration of death" removed. The Spirit takes away the blindness (the veil). The Holy Spirit had been promised (Acts 1:8). His presence was experienced on the day of Pentecost. This resulted in Peter saying, "Therefore being by the right hand of God exalted, and having received of the Father the promise of the Holy Ghost, he hath shed forth this, which ye now see and hear" (Acts 2:33). Writing to Titus, Paul said, "But after that the kindness and love of God our Saviour toward man appeared, Not by works of righteousness which we have done, but according to his mercy he saved us, by the washing of regeneration, and renewing of the Holy Ghost; Which he shed on us abundantly through Jesus Christ our Saviour" (Titus 3:4-6). Therefore, neither the Jew, nor the Gentile, can of himself see Christ as Savior and Redeemer. He needs the seeing power of the Holy Spirit. "And that no man can say that Jesus is the Lord, but by the Holy Ghost" (1 Corinthians 12:3). From this perspective Paul could say that the giving of the Spirit outshines the glory of the giving of the law just like the blazing sun outshines the light of the moon. If the momentous occasion of the giving of the law was glorious, then the giving of the Spirit of Christ, who takes the "veil" away, is far exceeding more glorious. "But we all, with open face beholding as in a glass the glory of the Lord, are changed into the same image from glory to glory, even as by the Spirit of the Lord" (2 Corinthians 3:18).

The Spirit of God can cut through the greatest blindness and enable the soul to see the light. The Jews, Paul claimed, were still blind (verses 14 and 15). The carnal mind is incapable of seeing the light of Christ. Paul says, "For we know that the law is spiritual: but I am carnal, sold under sin" (Romans 7:14). Therefore, the only way to become spiritual and live in harmony with the spirit of the law is through the Spirit. "That the righteousness of the law might be fulfilled in us, who walk not after the flesh, but after the Spirit. For they that are after the flesh do mind the things of the flesh; but they that are after the Spirit the things of the Spirit. For to be carnally minded is death; but to be spiritually minded is life and peace. Because the carnal mind is enmity against God: for it is not subject to the law of God, neither indeed can be. So then they that are in the flesh cannot please God. But ye are not in the flesh, but in the Spirit, if so be that the Spirit of God dwell in you" (Romans 8:4-9). Notice that to be carnally minded is "death." But only through the Spirit can a person be "spiritually minded."

It is fascinating to note that Pentecost was called the Feast of Harvest in the Old Testament. It was called Pentecost, from a Greek word meaning "fiftieth." Fifty days were to be numbered from the day the barley sheaf was offered (Leviticus 23:15–21). The fiftieth day was called the Feast of Weeks (Deuteronomy 16:10, 11) because seven full weeks separated it from the Passover. This feast was celebrated at the time of the spring harvest, which normally falls late in our month of May or early in June. It is calculated that the law was given just fifty days after the Israelites made their exodus out of Egypt (Exodus 19:1-16), in remembrance of which the Feast of Harvest was observed the fiftieth day after the Passover. The Holy Ghost was given on the Feast of Pentecost commemorating the giving of the law fifty days after the death of Christ, and by Him a harvest was gathered. In this sense, the outpouring of heaven's power in the person of the Spirit outshines the giving of the law. While the law only reveals sin and its consequences, the Spirit empowers the sinner to overcome sin and live in harmony with God's holy law.

2 Corinthians 4:16
For which cause we faint not; but though our outward man perish, yet the inward man is renewed day by day.

Answer
It does not matter how old a person becomes, his physical frame may continue to deteriorate, but his spiritual life may continue to increase from day to day. Paul states, "I die daily" (1 Corinthians 15:31). Though this statement can be viewed as speaking of the physical, Paul is talking about dying to self so he could live for Christ. Paul is constantly contrasting the spiritual with the physical. In Galatians he writes, "Walk in the Spirit, and ye shall not fulfill the lust of the flesh" (Galatians 5:16). Paul, in the verse in question, is talking about the inner strength he finds in the Lord. He writes, "And he said unto me, My grace is sufficient for thee: for my strength is made perfect in weakness. Most gladly therefore will I rather glory in my infirmities, that the power of Christ may rest upon me. Therefore I take pleasure in infirmities, in reproaches, in necessities, in persecutions, in distresses for Christ's sake: for when I am weak, then am I strong" (2 Corinthians 12:9, 10). And in Philippians he wrote, "I can do all things through Christ which strengtheneth me" (Philippians 4:13).

2 Corinthians 5:6-8
Therefore we are always confident, knowing that, whilst we are at home in the body, we are absent from the Lord (For we walk by faith, not by sight:) We are confident, I say, and willing rather to be absent from the body,

and to be present with the Lord.

Answer

There are only two known recorded cases of people who went directly to heaven without seeing death. They were Enoch (Hebrews 11:5) and Elijah (2 Kings 2:11). They were translated bodily to heaven. These two could not be absent from their bodies. Jesus himself was not absent from His body when He went to heaven. He told His disciples, "Behold my hands and my feet, that it is I myself: handle me, and see; for a spirit hath not flesh and bones, as ye see me have." Forty days later the disciples saw Him corporally ascend to heaven (Acts 1:9-11). Jesus did not promise translation for His own beloved disciples. Instead, He promised them that He would return to the earth to gather them (John 14:1-3). Jesus did not present them with the hope of death and immediate presence with the Lord. Rather, they were to rest here on earth until the glad day of the resurrection when the Lord would awaken them (1 Thessalonians 4:13-17).

The One who wrote 2 Corinthians also wrote 1 Corinthians. He vehemently argues the essential of a resurrection. He wrote: "And if Christ be not raised, your faith is vain; ye are yet in your sins. Then they also which are fallen asleep in Christ are perished. If in this life only we have hope in Christ, we are of all men most miserable. But now is Christ risen from the dead, and become the firstfruits of them that slept. For since by man came death, by man came also the resurrection of the dead. For as in Adam all die, even so in Christ shall all be made alive. But every man in his own order: Christ the firstfruits; afterward they that are Christ's at his coming" (1 Corinthians 15:17-23).

Notice that the hope of the resurrection will be realized

"at His coming." Paul had this hope himself. He wrote, "Knowing that he which raised up the Lord Jesus shall raise up us also by Jesus, and shall present us with you" (2 Corinthians 4:14). On one occasion, Paul was fearful that his life was about to end. Regarding this incident, the book of Acts records the episode. "For we would not, brethren, have you ignorant of our trouble which came to us in Asia, that we were pressed out of measure, above strength, insomuch that we despaired even of life: But we had the sentence of death in ourselves, that we should not trust in ourselves, but in God which raiseth the dead" (2 Corinthians 1:8, 9). Notice that Paul did not say that he was going directly to heaven at death, but rather that his hope was in the resurrection. To the Philippians he wrote, "That I may know him, and the power of his resurrection, and the fellowship of his sufferings, being made conformable unto his death; If by any means I might attain unto the resurrection of the dead" (Philippians 3:10-11).

Notice when Paul thought this "presence with the Lord" would be. "For what is our hope, or joy, or crown of rejoicing? Are not even ye in the presence of our Lord Jesus Christ at his coming?" (1 Thessalonians 2:19). Peter likewise had this hope. He wrote, "Blessed be the God and Father of our Lord Jesus Christ, which according to his abundant mercy hath begotten us again unto a lively hope by the resurrection of Jesus Christ from the dead, To an inheritance incorruptible, and undefiled, and that fadeth not away, reserved in heaven for you, Who are kept by the power of God through faith unto salvation ready to be revealed in the last time" (1 Peter 1:3-5).

It would be extremely incongruous to suppose that Christ would tell his chosen disciples that they would have to wait until His return before they could be with Him (see John 14:1-3; Acts 1:9-11), but allow Paul instant entrance into the kingdom. In Jesus' prayer in John chapter 17 he claimed that the father had given them (the disciples) to him. "As thou hast given him power over all flesh, that he should give eternal life to as many as thou hast given him. While I was with them in the world, I kept them in thy name: those that thou gavest me I have kept, and none of them is lost, but the son of perdition; that the scripture might be fulfilled" (John 17:2,12).

In John chapter 6, He declares that this eternal life is realized at the last day. We read: "And this is the Father's will which hath sent me, that of <u>all which he hath given me</u> I should lose nothing, but should <u>raise it up again at the last day</u>. And this is the will of him that sent me, that every one which seeth the Son, and believeth on him, <u>may have everlasting life: and I will raise him up at the last day</u>" (John 6:39, 40). Notice they will have to wait until He resurrects them when He returns in the last day. It is then that "this corruptible must put on incorruption, and this mortal must put on immortality," according to Paul's own words (see 1 Corinthians 15:53).

Even when seeking to encourage his fellow believers to endure in the face of hopelessness, he writes: "Being confident of this very thing, that he which hath begun a good work in you will perform it until the day of Jesus Christ" (Philippians 1:6). His hope of living beyond the present state of things, and hope of the believers would have to rest in the full assurance of the Lord's return.

2 Corinthians 12:2,3

I knew a man in Christ above fourteen years ago, (whether in the body, I cannot tell; or whether out of the body, I cannot tell: God knoweth;) such an one caught up to the third heaven. And I knew such a man, (whether in the body, or out of the body, I cannot tell: God knoweth;)

Answer

This language that Paul is using is modestly revealing a vision he had. While there are those that seek to employ this as support for the doctrine of the immortality of the soul, the text does not lend weight to such a twist. Second Corinthians was written in about A.D. 57; Paul died in A.D. 67. It is not possible that Paul was stating that his soul went to heaven, else he would have had to die in 57 A.D. He is speaking of "visions" and "revelations" found in verse one. His vision was so real that, like some dreams we have, it is difficult to tell that we are not literally there. He is not willing to boast about this fact, so he states, "For though I would desire to glory, I shall not be a fool" (verse 6). Paul uses the same language when writing to the Colossians. He wrote, "For though I be absent in the flesh, yet am I with you in the spirit, joying and beholding your order, and the stedfastness of your faith in Christ" (Colossians 2:5). Here he was simply expressing how he keeps track of them and rejoices over the good reports as if he were present.

In these verses he also introduces an interesting phrase. He says, "caught up to the third heaven." Then he replaces this phrase with "he was caught up into paradise" (verse 4). He is obviously stating that he had a vision of heaven and saw things that he was not permitted to speak about. It was this paradise that Christ himself promises to the thief on the cross. (See Luke 23:43). Later on in Revelation He says, "He that hath an ear, let him hear what the Spirit saith unto the churches; To him that overcometh will I give to eat of the tree of life, which is in the midst of the paradise of God" (Revelation 2:7). Where is this tree of life? In the "midst of the paradise of God." Notice that the promise is to "eat of the tree of life." In chapter 22 it says, "And he shewed me a pure river of water of life, clear as crystal, proceeding out of the throne of God and of the Lamb. In the midst of the street of it, and on either side of the river, was there the tree of life" (Revelation 22:1, 2). Paradise is where God is. This is why Paul is humble about what he was permitted to see.

Galatians 2:19

For I through the law am dead to the law,
that I might live unto God.

Answer

Being dead to the law means living in such a way that the law has nothing to condemn. To Paul, the law pointed out his sins (Romans 3:20). This resulted in leading him to Christ for cleansing (Romans 8:3). By dying to sin through Christ, he no longer was alive to sin, or in today's lingo, had no more desire to practice sin. Hence, he was dead to the law (Romans 7:4). In Romans chapter 6 he writes, "Knowing this, that our old man is crucified with him, that the body of sin might be destroyed, that henceforth we should not serve sin. For he that is dead is freed from sin. Now if we be dead with Christ, we believe that we shall also live with him: Knowing that Christ being raised from the dead dieth no more; death hath no more dominion over him. For in that he died, he died unto sin once: but in that he liveth, he liveth unto God. Likewise reckon ye also yourselves to be dead indeed unto sin, but alive unto God through Jesus Christ our Lord" (Romans 6:6-11).

Paul states that he is the one who dies, not the law. This death is to sin. In the proceeding verses of Romans chapter 6 he said, "What shall we say then? Shall we continue in sin, that grace may abound? God forbid. How shall we, that are dead to sin, live any longer therein? Know ye not, that so many of us as were baptized into Jesus Christ were baptized into his death? Therefore we are buried with him by baptism into death: that like as Christ was raised up from the dead by the glory of the Father, even so we also should walk in newness of life. For if we have been planted together in the likeness of his death, we shall be also in the likeness of his resurrection: Knowing this, that our old man is crucified with him, that the body of sin might be destroyed, that henceforth we should not serve sin. For he that is dead is freed from sin" (Romans 6:1-7). "But now we are delivered from the law, that being dead wherein we were held; that we should serve in newness of spirit, and not in the oldness of the letter. What shall we say then? Is the law sin? God forbid" (Romans 7:6, 7). The thief held in bondage to the evil desires of stealing is under the condemnation of the law—he is alive in sin and therefore under the sentence of the law. But when through Christ he becomes a "new creature," his carnal nature dies. He loses those carnal desires and no longer practices sin. He is therefore no longer subject to the charges of the law, just like a good law-abiding citizen is free from the law.

Galatians 3:19

Wherefore then serveth the law? It was added because of transgressions, till the seed should come to whom the promise was made; and it was ordained by angels in the hand of a mediator.

Answer

This law that Paul is speaking about in this chapter is obviously the ceremonial law, for it was given "four hundred and thirty years after" (verse 17). And it is called the "book of the law" (verse 10). It was the ceremonial law that was written in the "book." Moses was told to "take this book of the law, and put it in the side of the ark of the covenant of the LORD your God, that it may be there for a witness against thee" (Deuteronomy 31:26). The commandments existed four hundred years prior, for God said about Abraham, "Because that Abraham obeyed my voice, and kept my charge, my commandments, my statutes, and my laws" (Genesis 26:5). Obviously, when it comes to justification, no one can be justified before God by keeping any law, be it the Ten Commandments or the ceremonial, "for all have sinned" (Romans 3:23). Putting it simply, if from this present moment you could start doing everything perfect, you still have a penalty for your past sins. Your present perfect works cannot pay for your former transgressions. Therefore, the law will only serve to condemn your past sins, but it cannot do anything to change you. It is only Christ's death that can atone for your sins, and His perfect life imputed to you that can justify you (Romans 3:20-31). That's the seed spoken of in this verse, which is Christ (Galatians 3:16).

Galatians 3:23-25

But before faith came, we were kept under the law, shut up unto the faith which should afterwards be revealed. Wherefore the law was our schoolmaster to bring us unto Christ, that we might be justified by faith. But after that faith is come, we are no longer under a schoolmaster.

Answer

Paul here is writing to the Gentiles. He is explaining the role of faith that comes to them. He in no way is suggesting that "faith" came after the law. He records in the book of Hebrews chapter 11 all those in the Old Testament that exercised faith.

He begins with Abel, the first martyr, and ends with Samuel and the prophets. (See Hebrews 11.) He is explaining to them that the Jew, like himself, only thought salvation came by the deeds of the law, so they lived with an endless list of things to do in futility. However, when through the Holy Spirit they grasped this thing called "faith," they found relief from the toilsome burden of trying to save themselves. They then could see the ceremonial law as a tutor to lead then to the One that all those ceremonies really pointed to—Christ! So after accepting Christ, the ceremonial laws, completing their task, ended. (See Daniel 9:27 and Colossians 2:13-17.)

Galatians 4:8-10

Howbeit then, when ye knew not God, ye did service unto them which by nature are no gods. But now, after that ye have known God, or rather are known of God, how turn ye again to the weak and beggarly elements, whereunto ye desire again to be in bondage?
Ye observe days, and months, and times, and years.

Answer

In this church of Galatia there were Judaizers seeking to overturn Paul's work among the Gentiles. They were attempting to get the Gentiles to be circumcised (Galatians 5:2-11) and to follow the feast days of the Old Testament. (See Leviticus 23:4-44 for a list of these festivals.) These feasts which were also called "sabbaths", aside from the weekly Sabbaths (Leviticus. 23:38), were considered shadows (Colossians 2:17) pointing to Christ. They were to be in force until the time that the type would meet antitype, or as it says in chapter 3:24: "The law was our schoolmaster to bring us to Christ." In other words, Christ was our Passover. For example, Paul wrote, "For even Christ our passover is sacrificed for us:

Therefore let us keep the feast, not with old leaven, neither with the leaven of malice and wickedness; but with the unleavened bread of sincerity and truth" (1 Corinthians 5:7, 8). This is the way that a Christian is to keep the "feast."

For a Christian to keep the literal Passover is to deny that Christ died as the lamb. In actuality, no one today can keep these feast days. For in order to keep them, the animal sacrifices must be offered. Each feast day required specific offerings. Not even the Jews today are able to keep them as proscribed by the ceremonial law. In the book of Chronicles we read, "And to offer all burnt sacrifices unto the LORD in the sabbaths, in the new moons, and on the set feasts, by number, according to the order commanded unto them, continually before the LORD" (1 Chronicles 23:31). In our day, animal sacrifices are outlawed. And those who make an attempt to keep these ceremonial days are effectually betraying Christ as the true Messiah. These feast days were called "sabbaths" and were to be observed in their season (Leviticus 23:4). They were to be observed on specific dates. For example, "In the fourteenth day of the first month at even is the LORD'S passover" (Leviticus 23:5). This means that it could fall on Wednesday, Thursday, or Friday, depending on the year. But because they were called sabbaths, the people were enjoined to cease from work just as if it were the weekly Sabbath. (See Leviticus 23.)

It is these ceremonies that fell on their specific times and dates that Paul calls "beggarly elements." Christ instituted a change for keeping the Passover prior to His death so that it could be included in the new covenant. He said, "For this is the blood of the New Testament, which is shed for many for the remission of sins" (Matthew 26:28). Notice that this is the only ceremony carried over by Him into the new covenant. This ceremony is called the Lord's Supper today. Paul, under inspiration, states not a specific time any longer enjoined upon believers for keeping it, but "as often as you do it" (1 Corinthians 11:23-26). Titus put it this way: "Not giving heed to Jewish fables, and commandments of men, that turn from the truth" (Titus 1:13).

Galatians 4:22-24

For it is written, that Abraham had two sons, the one by a bondmaid, the other by a freewoman. But he who was of the bondwoman was born after the flesh; but he of the freewoman was by promise. Which things are an allegory: for these are the two covenants; the one from the mount Sinai, which gendereth to bondage, which is Agar.

Answer

Paul in allegorical language is comparing the two covenants — the old and the new. The one son, Isaac, was born in response to the faith in God's promise. The other son, Ishmael, came by Abraham's own efforts. One, Isaac, was considered the work of God, and the second, Ishmael, the work of man. The first took supernatural power to produce. The same is true with the spiritual regeneration. It is God that enables the sinner, through the mysterious power of grace, to overcome sin and be free. The first agreement (covenant) made by the Jews in Sinai was, "All that the Lord has spoken, we will do" (Exodus 19:8). But in their own strength, they could never. The new covenant is "Christ in you the hope of Glory" (Colossians 1:27). God has promised, "For this is the covenant that I will make with the house of Israel after those days, saith the Lord; I will put my laws into their mind, and write them in their hearts: and I will be to them a God, and they shall be to me a people: And they shall not teach every man his neighbour, and every man his brother, saying, Know the Lord: for all shall know me, from the least to the greatest. For I will be merciful to their unrighteousness, and their sins and their iniquities will I remember no more" (Hebrews 8:10-12). People who try to save themselves by their own works are like the bondwoman. People who find salvation in Christ are like Sarah experiencing the power of God to convert them into a new creature through faith.

Ephesians 2:15

Having abolished in his flesh the enmity, even the law of commandments contained in ordinances; for to make in himself of twain one new man, so making peace.

Answer

In brief, Paul is describing the enmity created by the law contained in ordinances, and the fact that Christ removes them. But notice that it is the "commandment contained in ordinances." These are the ordinances "according to the whole law and the statutes and the ordinances by the hand of Moses" (2 Chronicles 33:8). This language never pertained to the Ten Commandments. (See my comments on Colossians 2:14-17).

Ephesians 4:8-10

Wherefore he saith, When he ascended up on high, he led captivity captive, and gave gifts unto men. (Now that he ascended, what is it but that he also descended first into the lower parts of the earth? He that descended is the same also that ascended up far above all heavens, that he might fill all things.)

Answer

This text is usually combined with 1 Peter 3:18, 19 by some to prove that Christ went to preach to those in hell. Please read my comments on 1 Peter 3:18, 19. What is amazing is that at every funeral those that preach a place of torment never have anyone going there. They usually have the deceased go to the "pearly gates." On most tombstones is inscribed the words "rest in peace." So what is the meaning of this verse? This set of verses needs to be divided in order to explain them.

When Jesus ascended (Acts 1:9-11) He promised the Holy Spirit (Acts 1:4-8). All the spiritual gifts mentioned in this chapter in Ephesians come in the train with the gift of the Holy Ghost. But before He ascended, He first descended. Where to? "To the lower parts of the earth." The Psalmist uses the same terminology. "Because thou hast been my help, therefore in the shadow of thy wings will I rejoice. My soul followeth hard after thee: thy right hand upholdeth me. But those that seek my soul, to destroy it, shall go into the lower parts of the earth. They shall fall by the sword: they shall be a portion for foxes" (Psalm 63:7-10). Notice that the term is used to describe victims that are fallen by the sword, or killed. And since they are a "portion for foxes," this language simply means death. And, I should add, that there are no foxes in the supposed "hell."

Jesus said to the Jewish leaders, "For as Jonas was three days and three nights in the whale's belly; so shall the Son of man be three days and three nights in the heart of the earth" (Matthew 12:40). Jesus was metaphorically speaking of His death and resurrection. He said unto them, "Destroy this temple, and in three days I will raise it up. Then said the Jews, Forty and six years was this temple in building, and wilt thou rear it up in three days? But he spake of the temple of his body. When therefore he was risen from the dead, his disciples remembered that he had said this unto them; and they believed the scripture, and the word which Jesus had said" (John 2:19-22). Upon the death of Christ, He was placed in the earth, or what we call the grave. (See Luke 23:52-55.) Then as promised, He arose.

Paul in the text at hand is once more highlighting the fact that Christ broke the portals of the tomb. By His own power, He had victory over death. But He did something even more. When he died, the graves of some who slept were opened. Matthew writes, "Jesus, when he had cried again with a loud voice, yielded up the ghost. And the graves were opened, and many bodies of the saints which slept arose, And came out of the graves after his resurrection, and went into the holy city, and appeared unto many" (Matthew 27:50, 52-53). It was this group called "captives" or "a host of captives" that Jesus led into heaven when He ascended. This phrase comes from Psalm 68. "Thou hast ascended on high, thou has led a captivity captive: thou hast received gifts for men" (Psalm 68:18). Not only did He conquer the tomb, He gave spiritual gifts, delivered some who were captives of death and the grave, and took them as samples of the harvest to heaven.

Philippians 1:23
For I am in a strait betwixt two, having a desire to depart, and to be with Christ; which is far better:

Answer

Paul's clear understanding of the hope of the resurrection should be considered in order to properly understand this statement. As explained before (see comments on 2 Corinthians 5:6-8), he did not believe or teach that at death he would go immediately to heaven. In fact, when writing to Timothy he said, "For I am now ready to be offered, and the time of my departure is at hand. I have fought a good fight, I have finished my course, I have kept the faith: Henceforth there is laid up for me a crown of righteousness, which the Lord, the righteous judge, shall give me at that day: and not to me only, but unto all them also that love his appearing" (2

Timothy 4:6-8). Notice that Paul's hope rested in the coming of the Lord, and at that time receiving his crown along with others. He also wrote about the same hope to Titus. "Looking for that blessed hope, and the glorious appearing of the great God and our Saviour Jesus Christ" (Titus 2:13). To "depart" meant to die. Paul was weary, and the weight of the gospel lay heavily on his shoulders. While he loved his work, he also longed to be with his Savior. To him, death would hasten the day when he would be with the Lord.

Colossians 2:14-17

Blotting out the handwriting of ordinances that was against us, which was contrary to us, and took it out of the way, nailing it to his cross; And having spoiled principalities and powers, he made a shew of them openly, triumphing over them in it. Let no man therefore judge you in meat, or in drink, or in respect of an holyday, or of the new moon, or of the sabbath days: Which are a shadow of things to come; but the body is of Christ.

Answer

This is one of the key texts used by antinomians to try and establish the point that the moral law was nailed to the cross. But it is not reasonable to suppose that the standard of righteousness, or the commandments by which man will be judged, could be done away with. (See Ecclesiastes 12:13, 14; James 2:10-12.) The Psalmist wrote, "Blessed is the man that walketh not in the counsel of the ungodly, nor standeth in the way of sinners, nor sitteth in the seat of the scornful. But his delight is in the law of the LORD; and in his law doth he meditate day and night" (Psalm 1:1, 2). "The law of the LORD is perfect, converting the soul: the testimony of the LORD is sure, making wise the simple. Moreover by them is thy

servant warned: and in keeping of them there is great reward"
(Psalm 19:7, 11). (See also Psalm 119, the psalm of the law.)

So what is the meaning of these verses? First of all, there are
several sets of laws in the Old Testament. There is the civil
law (an eye for an eye), health laws (diet and sanitation),
the moral law (Ten Commandments), and the ceremonial
law (feast days and sacrifices). A careful look at the words
in these verses will help to distinguish which sets of laws
Paul is speaking about. Notice that it says, "Handwriting of
ordinances that was against us." It is not the moral law that was
"against us," for the Bible says, "And the LORD commanded
us to do all these statutes, to fear the LORD our God, for our
good always, that he might preserve us alive, as it is at this
day. And it shall be our righteousness, if we observe to do all
these commandments before the LORD our God, as he hath
commanded us" (Deuteronomy 6:24-25). "The tables were the
work of God, and the writing was the writing of God, graven
upon the tables" (Exodus 32:16; Deuteronomy 9:9, 10). When
Moses broke the tablets, God told him to bring again two new
tablets, and God rewrote them (Deuteronomy 9:9, 10). This
law was placed inside the ark. God said, "And I will write on
the tables the words that were in the first tables which thou
brakest, and thou shalt put them in the ark (Deuteronomy 10:2).

The ceremonial law, on the other hand, was "against us."
God told Moses, "Take this book of the law, and put it in the
side of the ark of the covenant of the LORD your God, that
it may be there for a witness against thee" (Deuteronomy
31:26). Notice that it is placed in the "side of the ark." On
the other hand, the Ten Commandments were placed inside
the ark. (See Deuteronomy 10:2-5.) This book of the law
contained the law with sabbaths, new moons, and meat and

drink offerings. On these specific days, specific meat, drink, and sacrificial offerings were to be made. "And to offer all burnt sacrifices unto the LORD in the sabbaths, in the new moons, and on the set feasts, by number, according to the order commanded unto them, continually before the LORD" (1 Chronicles 23:31). These feast days were called "sabbaths" because they were to be observed as the Sabbath (Leviticus 23:24, 25). In simpler language, when they heard a day called a sabbath, it was a day for religious activities only. However, they were not the weekly Sabbaths of the fourth commandment. These were to be observed in their season (Leviticus 23:4). This is the law that pointed to Christ and was nailed to the cross. Notice that God said, "Bring no more vain oblations; incense is an abomination unto me; the new moons and sabbaths, the calling of assemblies, I cannot away with; it is iniquity, even the solemn meeting" (Isaiah 1:13).

While Isaiah was inspired to write that these sabbaths would be removed, in chapter 66 he writes about sabbaths that are eternal. "For as the new heavens and the new earth, which I will make shall remain before me, saith the Lord, so shall your seed and your name remain. And it shall come to pass, that from one new moon to another, and from one Sabbath to another, shall all flesh come to worship before me, saith the Lord" (Isaiah 66:22, 23). Notice that one passes, but the other will continue throughout eternity. Hosea also writes about the termination of the ceremonies. "I will also cause all her mirth to cease, her feast days, her new moons, and her sabbaths, and all her solemn feasts" (Hosea 2:11). These are the feasts predicted to be done away with. Daniel confirms the same: "And he shall confirm the covenant with many for one week: and in the midst of the week he shall cause the sacrifice and the oblation to cease" (Daniel 9:27). These predictions met their fulfillment at the cross when the "veil of the temple was rent in twain from the top to the bottom," bringing an end to the sacrificial system. (See Matthew 27:51, 52.)

Because the ceremonial laws were done away with, no one is to judge you in "meat" offerings, or in "drink" offerings, or in respect of a ceremonial "holy day," or of the "new moon," or of the ceremonial "sabbath days," which were a shadow of things to come by nailing them to the cross. Christ was the substance that cast the shadow. The shadow in turn pointed to him.

1 Thessalonians 3:13

To the end he may stablish your hearts unblameable in holiness before God, even our Father, at the coming of our Lord Jesus Christ with all his saints.

Answer

Biblically speaking, saints can be humans or angels. In this case, Paul is referring to angels. This is in harmony with the words of Christ: "So shall it be at the end of the world: the angels shall come forth, and sever the wicked from among the just" (Matthew 13:49). "For the Son of man shall come in the glory of his Father with his angels; and then he shall reward every man according to his works" (Matthew 16:27). "When the Son of man shall come in his glory, and all the holy angels with him, then shall he sit upon the throne of his glory" (Matthew 25:31). Jude writes about the Lord's coming in this manner: "Behold, the Lord cometh with ten thousands of his saints" (Jude 14). The same language is found when God gave his commandments on Sinai. Moses wrote, "The LORD came from Sinai, and rose up from Seir unto them; he shined forth from mount Paran, and he came with ten thousands of saints: from his right hand went a fiery law for them" (Deuteronomy

33:2). Daniel writes, "A fiery stream issued and came forth from before him: thousand thousands ministered unto him, and ten thousand times ten thousand stood before him: the judgment was set, and the books were opened" (Daniel 7:10). And the revelator wrote, "I beheld, and I heard the voice of many angels round about the throne and the beasts and the elders: and the number of them was ten thousand times ten thousand, and thousands of thousands" (Revelation 5:11).

It is clear from these verses that angels are called saints, and it is they that will accompany their Lord on the greatest rescue mission undertaken. Never in the scriptures are human beings mentioned as coming back with Christ. Even the disciples were told they would have to wait until the Lord returned to receive them and take them to where He is (John 14:1-3). This promise will be consummated when the "Lord descends from heaven … and the dead in Christ shall rise first" (1 Thessalonians 4:13-17).

1 Thessalonians 4:14

For if we believe that Jesus died and rose again, even so them also which sleep in Jesus will God bring with him.

Answer

At a surface reading this verse seems to imply that the righteous come back with Jesus. But a correct understanding of the verse is rendered by the next verses. Let's take a look at verses 13 through 17. "But I would not have you to be ignorant, brethren, concerning them which are asleep, that ye sorrow not, even as others which have no hope. For if we believe that Jesus died and rose again, even so them also which sleep in Jesus will God bring with him. For this we say unto you by the word of the Lord, that we which are alive and remain unto the coming of the Lord shall not prevent them which are asleep. For the Lord himself shall descend from heaven with a shout, with the voice of the archangel, and with the trump of God: and the dead in Christ shall rise first: Then we which are alive and remain shall be caught up together with them in the clouds, to meet the Lord in the air: and so shall we ever be with the Lord" (1 Thessalonians 4:13-17).

Take special note that Paul is speaking about those that "sleep in Jesus." This phrase he, as well as Christ, uses when referring to the dead in Christ. (See John 11:11-14; 1 Corinthians 15:13, 18.) Those who are "asleep in Jesus" are raised when he comes. Therefore, how can they be coming from Heaven with Christ when in reality they awake from their sleep in the graves at His coming? "This is the will of him that sent me, that every one which seeth the Son, and believeth on him, may have everlasting life: and I will raise him up at the last day" (John 6:39). He repeated the words "at the last day" in verses 40, 44, and 54. The whole of Paul's counsel is to comfort those who have lost loved ones through death and are buried. If the loved ones were in heaven already, there would be no need for these verses, and no need for sorrow. So, just as Jesus rose again, so the same way will God "bring" with Him or raise with Him those that are dead. When Jesus descends to gather His sleeping saints, then God will bring (or raise with Jesus) those who have been resurrected.

1 Thessalonians 5:2; 2 Peter 3:10

For yourselves know perfectly that the day of the Lord so cometh as a thief in the night." "But the day of the Lord will come as a thief in the night; in the which the heavens shall pass away with a great noise, and the elements shall melt with fervent heat, the earth also and the works that are therein shall be burned up.

Answer

These two texts have to do with the "element of surprise." Jesus uses the same illustration. He said: "And this know, that if the goodman of the house had known what hour the thief would come, he would have watched, and not have suffered his house to be broken through. Be ye therefore ready also: for the Son of man cometh at an hour when ye think not" (Luke 12:39, 40). Notice that Jesus is stressing the need to watch so as to avoid discovering after the fact that a thief has come.

A thief does not announce his approach. It is after the event that the victim realizes he has suffered from the crook's prowess. The same is true with this analogy. By using this illustration Christ is not calling himself a thief. Neither is he suggesting that the victim disappears when the thief comes. The victim must be present and be around after the fact in order for the illustration to be complete. Christ is simply advocating the essential of being in a state of readiness so that when He comes, it will not catch the watcher by surprise.

Some use the "thief in the night" phrase to support the idea of people disappearing instantly at an unannounced moment. The problem with this is simply that in both instances of the texts in consideration the thought does not end there. In 1 Thessalonians it says: "For when they shall say, Peace and safety; then sudden destruction cometh upon them, as travail upon a woman with child; and they shall not escape. But ye, brethren, are not in darkness, that that day should overtake you as a thief" (verses 3, 4). Notice that the same is true here. Those who are watching will not be taken by surprise. Peter, when referring to the same illustration, concludes with the words: "in the which the heavens shall pass away with a great noise, and the elements shall melt with fervent heat, the earth also and the works that are therein shall be burned up." Please take notice that nothing remains once the "thief" (suggesting the end of all things comes suddenly). Instead, the earth burns up! So, be ready! That's the message.

1 Thessalonians 5:23

And the very God of peace sanctify you wholly; and I pray God your whole spirit and soul and body be preserved blameless unto the coming of our Lord Jesus Christ.

Answer

This text deserves explanation because it seems to suggest that man is made up of three entities. Usually those who teach the immortality of the soul purport that man is made of two entities, while Paul mentions three. Why? With these words, he is seeking to make sure that no part of his reader's life is left untouched by God's transforming, sanctifying power. Biblically speaking, the scriptures only speak of a twofold division in man, either body and soul, or body and spirit. In Thessalonians Paul divides man into three. It is important to clarify at this point that in the entire Bible the words "soul" or "spirit" are never considered to be immortal, imperishable, unending.

By this word "spirit" (*pneuma* in Greek) he is speaking of the higher principle of intelligence and thought with which man is endowed. This same word is used when Jesus is troubled at heart over certain situations. (See John 11:33; 13:21.) No one believes that Jesus has a separate spirit. It is through the higher regents of our intelligence that God can communicate by His Spirit. (See Romans 8:16.) It is by the renewing of the "spirit" through the action of the Holy Spirit that the individual is changed and sanctified into Christ's likeness. (See Romans 12:1, 2.) That is why Paul can say, "Therefore if any man be in Christ, he is a new creature: old things are passed away; behold, all things are become new" (2 Corinthians 5:17).

The word "soul" (*psuchep* in Greek) is translated 40 times in the New Testament as "life" or "lives." It is that part of a man's nature that finds expression through the desires, emotions, and natural impulses. This part of one's nature must be sanctified as well. Paul compares the higher nature, "the spirit," with the lower nature, the "flesh" (Galatians 5:16-26). In order to be sanctified, these parts of the being must be brought into conformity with the mind of God. This can be done only through the Holy Spirit. Sanctified human reason then controls the lower nature, the impulses, which would otherwise be contrary to God. By this means, the will becomes subject to the will of God, and thereby reach that sanctification that makes a person "whole" and "preserved blameless unto the coming of our Lord Jesus Christ.

The meaning of "body" (*soµma* in Greek) is obvious. It is the flesh, blood, and bones. This part is controlled by either the higher or the lower nature. Paul says, "But I keep under my body, and bring it into subjection" (1 Corinthians 9:27). When the mind is sanctified, the body can also be sanctified. In order for sanctification to be complete, the body must be included. Why? Because our body is to be the temple of God's indwelling (1 Corinthians 6:19, 20).

2 Thessalonians 2:6
And now ye know what withholdeth
that he might be revealed in his time.

Answer

Paul is speaking of the antichrist and its rise. (See

verses 3 and 4.) But before it can rise, whatever power "withholdeth" or is holding it back will first have to be removed. Paul reminds the Thessalonian believers that he had told them before, but is not at liberty at this point to write concerning who or what the power may be.

2 Thessalonians 2:15
Therefore, brethren, stand fast, and hold the traditions which ye have been taught, whether by word, or our epistle.

Answer
Paul had already underscored the essentiality of the Bible as the sole rule of faith. In chapter 3 he says, "Pray for us, that the word of the Lord may have free course and be glorified" (2 Thessalonians 3:1). Based on this, he adds, "we have confidence in the Lord touching you, that ye both do and will do the things which we command you" (verse 3). The "traditions," such as the Lord's Supper, or that which was handed to them, is set forth by the example of the apostles (2 Thessalonians 3:7-14) and by the "command" and exhortation by the Lord Jesus Christ. (See 2 Thessalonians 3:12.)

1 Timothy 2:11-15
Let the woman learn in silence with all subjection. But I suffer not a woman to teach, nor to usurp authority over the man, but to be in silence. For Adam was first formed, then Eve. And Adam was not deceived, but the woman being deceived was in the transgression. Notwithstanding she shall be saved in childbearing, if they continue in faith and charity and holiness with sobriety.

Answer
For Paul to have written this suggests that there was seen an imbalance in the role of men and women in the church.

He is saying that woman ought not to speak in the church. First, along with "man praying or prophesying (1 Corinthians 11:4), he adds "women that prayeth or prophesieth" (verse 5). Philip the evangelist (Acts 21:8) "had four daughters, virgins, which did prophesy" (Acts 21:9). According to Paul's own counsel, prophesying was to be done in the church (1 Corinthians 14:23, 24). Therefore, if these virgins were prophetesses, then it is obvious that they would prophesy in the church. Anna the prophetess was in the temple when Jesus was being dedicated. She spoke in the temple. It says, "And there was one Anna, a prophetess, the daughter of Phanuel, of the tribe of Aser: she was of a great age, and had lived with an husband seven years from her virginity; And she was a widow of about fourscore and four years, which departed not from the temple, but served God with fastings and prayers night and day. And she coming in that instant gave thanks likewise unto the Lord, and spake of him to all them that looked for redemption in Jerusalem" (Luke 2:36-38).

Paul's concern then is to set proper order in both 1 Corinthians 14:34-35 and the text here in question relative to the role of man and wife. Man, as in the case of Adam, should have the authority, not the woman. The woman is to be in subjection to the husband, not the husband to the wife. Peter writes the same counsel. He wrote, "Likewise, ye wives, be in subjection to your own husbands; that, if any obey not the word, they also may without the word be won by the conversation of the wives" (2 Peter 3:1).

1 Timothy 4:1-5

Now the Spirit speaketh expressly, that in the latter times some shall depart from the faith, giving heed to seducing spirits, and doctrines of devils; Speaking lies in hypocrisy; having their conscience seared with a hot iron; Forbidding to

marry, and commanding to abstain from meats, which God
hath created to be received with thanksgiving of them which
believe and know the truth. For every creature of God is good,
and nothing to be refused, if it be received with thanksgiving:
For it is sanctified by the word of God and prayer.

Answer

This text warns about those who depart from the faith. But how do they depart from the faith? They forbid to marry, and to abstain from food which God created. God gave both marriage and food in the beginning. In Genesis 1:29, "God said, Behold, I have given you every herb bearing seed, which is upon the face of all the earth, and every tree, in the which is the fruit of a tree yielding seed; to you it shall be for meat." And in Genesis 2:21-25 the first marriage is recorded. "And Adam said, This is now bone of my bones, and flesh of my flesh: she shall be called Woman, because she was taken out of Man. Therefore shall a man leave his father and his mother, and shall cleave unto his wife: and they shall be one flesh. And they were both naked, the man and his wife, and were not ashamed." The admonition is given to bring to light those who encourage celibacy, and abstain from the food that was part of the God-given diet. Since this food is sanctified (set apart for a holy use) by the word of God and prayer, then it stands to reason that those who try to lead away from divine counsel are considered to be giving "heed to seducing spirits." The phrase "every creature" in the Greek is "things created." The food approved in the word of God is found in Genesis 1:29; 3:18; and Leviticus 11. These texts contain the type of things God has set aside for food. Anyone that contradicts this is fulfilling the warning of Paul.

1 Timothy 5:23

*Drink no longer water, but use a little wine
for thy stomach's sake and thine often infirmities.*

Answer

It is obvious from the counsel of Paul to his spiritual son Timothy that he was suffering from stomach problems. Paul is not suggesting that Timothy no longer drink any water. But rather, that he not drink water for his stomach's problem, but instead use a little wine. Since Paul was acquainted with the Bible's injunction concerning alcoholic liquors (Proverbs 20:1 and 23:29-32), and since Timothy was not considered as "ready to perish" or "of heavy hearts" (Proverbs 31:4-7), it would be unthinkable that the experienced missionary is suggesting that he imbibe. Rather, he was saying, "Drink grape juice for your stomach's sake." Recent studies show that "Purple grape juice contains the same powerful disease-fighting antioxidants, called flavonoids, that are believed to give wine many of its heart-friendly benefits" (CNN report, *Wine or Welch's? Grape Juice Provides Health Benefits Without Alcohol.* March 31, 2000).

Titus 1:15

*Unto the pure all things are pure: but unto them that are defiled and unbelieving is nothing pure;
but even their mind and conscience is defiled.*

Answer

The pure-minded person, generally speaking, has an innocent way of looking at things, while the "defiled and unbelieving" translate matters into an impure perspective. This of course does not mean that a Christian calls sin pure. God warns about calling sin by its rightful name. Paul writes, "Wherefore the law is holy, and the commandment holy, and just, and good. Was then that which is good made death unto me? God forbid. But sin, that it might appear sin, working death in me by that which is good; that sin by the commandment might become exceeding sinful" (Romans 7:12). A Christian should be able to judge between that which is true and that which is false. God says, "Beloved, believe not every spirit, but try the spirits whether they are of God: because many false prophets are gone out into the world" (1 John 4:1). And the role of the leader is to teach to discriminate between the pure and the defiled. Ezekiel wrote, "Her priests have violated my law, and have profaned mine holy things: they have put no difference between the holy and profane, neither have they shewed difference between the unclean and the clean, and have hid their eyes from my sabbaths, and I am profaned among them. And they shall teach my people the difference between the holy and profane, and cause them to discern between the unclean and the clean" (Ezekiel 22:26; 44:23). Jesus warned, "Ye shall know them by their fruits" (Matthew 7:16).

Hebrews 8:7, 8

For if that first covenant had been faultless, then should no place have been sought for the second. For finding fault with them, he saith, Behold, the days come, saith the Lord, when I will make a new covenant with the house of Israel and with the house of Judah:

Answer

Of all the references used to try and make of none effect the law of God, this is the one most often used. Yet when understood, it says the opposite of what dispensationalists teach. First of all, a covenant is an agreement between two persons. In this case, God and the Israelites entered into a mutual agreement. This is described in Exodus 19:5-8. The covenant and the law are two separate things. Referring to this fact, in the book of Chronicles we read, "There was nothing in the ark save the two tables which Moses put therein at Horeb, when the Lord made a covenant with the children of Israel, when they came out of Egypt (2 Chronicles 5:10). The agreement was based upon the principles of the law. In this agreement, the people promised to be loyal to Him, showing this loyalty by keeping His Ten Commandments. It was confirmed by the sprinkling of animal blood (Exodus 24:7, 8). But the problem was that though God kept His part of the deal, "they continued not in my covenant" (Hebrews 8:9).

God said concerning their betrayal of the relationship, "Thus saith the LORD, Where is the bill of your mother's divorcement, whom I have put away? or which of my creditors is it to whom I have sold you? Behold, for your iniquities have ye sold yourselves, and for your transgressions is your mother put away" (Isaiah 50:1, 2). "My covenant they brake, although I was an husband unto them, saith the LORD" (Jeremiah 31:32). So the old covenant had poor promises (verse 6), was faulty (verse 7), and waxed old and vanished away (verse 13). Notice that the old covenant was like a marriage agreement that the people, not God, defected in. When someone in a marriage relationship commits adultery, it is the covenant that is broken; the principles that contribute to a happy marriage still remain.

On the other hand, the new covenant was given without the human agent promising anything. It was offered by Christ, and made sure with His blood (Matthew 26:28; Hebrews 12:24; 13:20). God had promised, "Behold, the days come, saith the LORD, that I will make a new covenant with the house of Israel, and with the house of Judah: Not according to the covenant that I made with their fathers in the day that I took them by the hand to bring them out of the land of Egypt;

which my covenant they brake, although I was an husband unto them, saith the LORD: But this shall be the covenant that I will make with the house of Israel; After those days, saith the LORD, I will put my law in their inward parts, and write it in their hearts; and will be their God, and they shall be my people. And they shall teach no more every man his neighbour, and every man his brother, saying, Know the LORD: for they shall all know me, from the least of them unto the greatest of them, saith the LORD: for I will forgive their iniquity, and I will remember their sin no more" (Jeremiah 31:31-34).

This covenant went into effect when Christ died. "For a testament is of force after men are dead: otherwise it is of no strength at all while the testator liveth" (Hebrews 9:17). However, once the testator dies, the testament cannot be changed. "Brethren, I speak after the manner of men; Though it be but a man's covenant, yet if it be confirmed, no man disannulleth, or addeth thereto" (Galatians 3:15). This means that once Christ died, anything instituted prior to His death is binding, and after His death nothing could be added or altered. That's why He said to His disciples, "If you love me, keep my commandments" (John 14:15). This precludes Sunday keeping, which came in after the resurrection of Christ. He also instituted the Lord's Supper prior to His death. That is why Christians keep it. (See 1 Corinthians 11:23-26.) By divine grace God has promised to all who would let Him, to write His laws in their hearts and minds. They are invited to enter into a covenant relationship with Him. Hence, His laws will be enshrined in the hearts of His people forever.

Hebrews 10:8, 9

Above when he said, Sacrifice and offering and burnt offerings and offering for sin thou wouldest not, neither hadst

pleasure therein; which are offered by the law; Then said he,
Lo, I come to do thy will, O God. He taketh away the first,
that he may establish the second.

Answer

These verses are taken from a quote in the Old Testament. Here is the full text: "Then said I, Lo, I come: in the volume of the book it is written of me, I delight to do thy will, O my God: yea, thy law is within my heart" (Psalm 40:7, 8). This is a prophecy concerning the Messiah and His attitude toward the Torah. Concerning this Jesus said, "As the Father hath loved me, so have I loved you: continue ye in my love. If ye keep my commandments, ye shall abide in my love; even as I have kept my Father's commandments, and abide in his love" (John 15:9, 10). The heart, in which Christ dwells, will have the same attitude toward that law. "For this is the love of God, that we keep his commandments: and his commandments are not grievous" (1 John 5:3). Paul explains what love is in this way, "Owe no man any thing, but to love one another: for he that loveth another hath fulfilled the law. For this, Thou shalt not commit adultery, Thou shalt not kill, Thou shalt not steal, Thou shalt not bear false witness, Thou shalt not covet; and if there be any other commandment, it is briefly comprehended in this saying, namely, Thou shalt love thy neighbour as thyself " (Romans 13:8, 9).

It is the sacrifices and burnt offerings that are taken away, which were part of the first covenant. These sacrifices and offerings are mentioned in the book of Chronicles. "Then Solomon offered burnt offerings unto the LORD on the altar of the LORD, which he had built before the porch, Even after a certain rate every day, offering according to the commandment of Moses, on the sabbaths, and on the new moons, and on the solemn feasts, three times in the year, even in the feast of unleavened bread, and in the feast of weeks, and in the feast of tabernacles" (2 Chronicles 8:12, 13). Notice that they were offered according to the commandment of Moses. The law in the heart of Christ was part of the new covenant. It is this delight about the law that Christ wants to instill in every believer.

Hebrews 12:22-24

But ye are come unto mount Sion, and unto the city of the living God, the heavenly Jerusalem, and to an innumerable company of angels, To the general assembly and church of the firstborn, which are written in heaven, and to God the Judge of all, and to the spirits of just men made perfect, And to Jesus the mediator of the new covenant, and to the blood of sprinkling, that speaketh better things than that of Abel.

Answer

Paul is speaking in allegorical terms. He is contrasting the new covenant with the old. Paul had mentioned Abel making a better sacrifice then Cain (Hebrews 11:4). Here he says that Jesus' mediation and sprinkling His blood (Hebrews 9:13, 14) is even better than that. The new covenant makes the "spirits of men perfect" because Christ writes His laws in their hearts. The new covenant is compared to coming to Mt. Zion, the "city of the living God, the heavenly Jerusalem," in contrast to Mt. Sinai of the old covenant. It is like coming to the "general assembly," literally, "festal gathering," to the church of the firstborn. That is, church of first-born ones, here referring to born-again Christians, which make up the invisible church. "Written in heaven," or "recorded in heaven," that is, in the Lamb's book of life (see Philippians 4:3; Revelation 3:5), as contrasting the hand written ordinances in a book (Deuteronomy 31:24-26). At Mt. Sinai the people were afraid and did not want to listen to God (Exodus 20:18-21). In the new covenant we can come directly before God the Judge. Jesus was the lawgiver at Mt. Sinai; on Mt. Zion He appears as "the Judge of all" men. Through Christ we can go to God with confidence.

1 Peter 3:18-20

For Christ also hath once suffered for sins, the just for the unjust, that he might bring us to God, being put to death in the flesh, but quickened by the Spirit: By which also he went and preached unto the spirits in prison; Which sometime were disobedient, when once the longsuffering of God waited in the days of Noah, while the ark was a preparing, wherein few, that is, eight souls were saved by water.

Answer

The use of this text to prove that Christ went down to hell and preached to the dead is most unfortunate. The wording is clear! It says, "Christ was put to death, but quickened by the Spirit." Then it says, "by which also he went and preached." The preaching, is done "by the 'Spirit" When was this preaching done? "In the days of Noah, while the ark was a preparing" (verse 20). In Genesis it says, "My Spirit shall not always strive with man" (Genesis 6:3). The term "spirits in prison" is an expression used in the Bible concerning people who are in bondage to sin. David pleads, "Bring my soul out of prison, that I may praise thy name: the righteous shall compass me about; for thou shalt deal bountifully with me" (Psalm 142:7). Concerning the work of the coming Messiah, Isaiah writes, "To open the blind eyes, to bring out the prisoners from the prison, and them that sit in darkness out of the prison house" (Isaiah 42:7). "The Spirit of the Lord GOD is upon me; because the LORD hath anointed me to preach good tidings unto the meek; he hath sent me to bind up the brokenhearted, to proclaim liberty to the captives, and the opening of the prison to them that are bound" (Isaiah 61:1). The word "prison" is used here in a figurative sense. It is used in the sense of being in bondage to sin. In Isaiah 42:22-24, the prophet pictures all the people as being "hid in prison houses."

Christ speaks of the bondage of sin. He said to the Jewish leaders, "And ye shall know the truth, and the truth shall make you free. They answered Him, "We be Abraham's seed, and were never in bondage to any man: how sayest thou, Ye shall be made free? Jesus answered them, Verily, verily, I say unto you, Whosoever committeth sin is the servant of sin" (John 8:32, 33). Peter's message is that the gospel was preached by Christ through the Holy Spirit to those in the bondage of sin during Noah's day.

1 Peter 4:6

For for this cause was the gospel preached also to them that are dead, that they might be judged according to men in the flesh, but live according to God in the spirit.

Answer

Peter again is stressing the point that the gospel had been "preached" (past tense) to those who had passed away. There are two categories of candidates for the judgment—the "quick," which means the living, and the dead—the meaning here is obvious (verse 5). If the dead were to be judged, it would only be fair if the gospel had already been given to them. When the gospel is preached to a person, the choice must be exercised either to continue to live in the flesh, as Peter reveals the Gentiles do (verse 3), or live in the spirit. "That he no longer should live the rest of his time in the flesh to the lusts of men, but to the will of God" (verse 2).

Peter is following the train of thought from chapter 3 concerning those that Christ had preached to and were dead.

2 Peter 2:4

For if God spared not the angels that sinned, but cast them down to hell, and delivered them into chains of darkness, to be reserved unto judgment;

Answer

From the encounters that Christ had with demons while on earth (See Matthew 4:24; 8:16; Mark 5:9, 10), there is evidence that the devils are not confined to a literal place and held in chains until the judgment. So, what is the meaning of this text? The Greek word for "hell" in this verse is *tartaroo*. This word is only found in this verse. The word normally used for the burning hell is *gehenna*. From this text it is difficult to extrapolate a place of burning for these angels. The text says that they are delivered "into chains of darkness." The same language is found in the book of Jude. It says, "And the angels which kept not their first estate, but left their own habitation, he hath reserved in everlasting chains under darkness unto the judgment of the great day" (Jude 6). These angels had dwelt in the presence of God's glory. When they rebelled against God, they were cast to the earth.

The revelator wrote: "And there was war in heaven: Michael and his angels fought against the dragon; and the dragon fought and his angels, And prevailed not; neither was their place found any more in heaven. And the great dragon was cast out, that old serpent, called the Devil, and Satan, which deceiveth the whole world: he was cast out into the earth, and his angels were cast out with him" (Revelation 12:7-9). Notice that the "darkness" is where they are held, not in torment of flames, or torture—they are not being punished but are reserved for the judgment. This judgment is rendered when the devil and his angels are cast "into everlasting fire, prepared for the devil and his angels" (Matthew 25:41). (See Revelation 20:11-15.)

2 Peter 3:8

But, beloved, be not ignorant of this one thing,
that one day is with the Lord as a thousand years,
and a thousand years as one day.

Answer

This language Peter is borrowing from the Old Testament. It says, "For a thousand years in thy sight are but as yesterday when it is past, and as a watch in the night" (Psalm 90:4). Peter is not saying, as some attempt to from this text, that a day is a thousand years. This statement is made in relationship to people that do not believe in the certainty of the coming of Christ. But they are ignorant of the fact that to God a thousand years is but a moment, and man's life, though he live to be a hundred, to God is but a day. God is not limited to time! Again in Psalm 90, the Psalmist says, "Before the mountains were brought forth, or ever thou hadst formed the earth and the world, even from everlasting to everlasting, thou art God. For a thousand years in thy sight are but as yesterday when it is past, and as a watch in the night. Thou carriest them away as with a flood; they are as a sleep: in the morning they are like grass which groweth up. In the morning it flourisheth, and groweth up; in the evening it is cut down, and withereth" (Psalm 90:2, 4-6). Peter confirms the fact that God is coming by stating, "The Lord is not slack concerning his promise, as some men count slackness; but is longsuffering to us-ward, not willing that any should perish, but that all should come to repentance. But the day of the Lord will come as a thief in the night; in the which the heavens shall pass away with a great noise, and the elements shall melt with fervent heat, the earth also and the works that are therein shall be burned up" (2 Peter 3:9, 10).

1 John 3:9

Whosoever is born of God doth not commit sin; for his seed remaineth in him: and he cannot sin, because he is born of God.

Answer

This passage of Scripture has troubled many sincere Christians striving to please God. They recognize that they sin while professing to serve Him. And the questions arise, "Am I really serving God?" Am I really converted?

The answer lies in 1 John 2:1. Notice that it says: "My little children, these things write I unto you, that ye sin not. And if any man sin, we have an advocate with the Father, Jesus Christ the righteous." The admonition is not to sin, but in the event that you do, there is an advocate—the only One who can defend you. And in 1 John 1:9 it says, "If we confess our sins, he is faithful and just to forgive us our sins, and to cleanse us from all unrighteousness."

So what is John saying by the text in question? He is admonishing the believers not to premeditate sinful acts, or habitually live in sin. It is one thing to mistakenly fall into sin; it is another thing to practice it. That is why he writes: "He that saith, I know him, and keepeth not his commandments, is a liar, and the truth is not in him. But whoso keepeth his word, in him verily is the love of God perfected: hereby know we that we are in him. He that saith he abideth in him ought himself also so to walk, even as he walked" (1 John 2:4-6). Paul puts it this way: "What shall we say then? Shall we continue in sin, that grace may abound? God forbid. How shall we, that are dead to sin, live any longer therein?" (Romans 6:1,2).

1 John 5:12

He that hath the Son hath life;
and he that hath not the Son of God hath not life.

Answer

A person who lives has life, but it is a temporal one. He will die. But the life John is speaking of here is the eternal life. In verse 11 it says, "And this is the record, that God hath given to us eternal life, and this life is in his Son." Jesus said, "I am the resurrection, and the life: he that believeth in me, though he were dead, yet shall he live" (John 11:25). In His prayer Christ said, "As thou hast given him power over all flesh, that he should give eternal life to as many as thou hast given him. And this is life eternal, that they might know thee the only true God, and Jesus Christ, whom thou hast sent" (John 17:2,3). Jesus told His deisciples, "Whoso eateth my flesh, and drinketh my blood, hath eternal life; and I will raise him up at the last day" (John 6:54). Please notice that this eternal life begins here when a person accepts Christ as their Lord and Savior, but will finally be realized "at the last trump: for the trumpet shall sound, and the dead shall be raised incorruptible, and we shall be changed. For this corruptible must put on incorruption, and this mortal must put on immortality. So when this corruptible shall have put on incorruption, and this mortal shall have put on immortality, then shall be brought to pass the saying that is written, Death is swallowed up in victory. O death, where is thy sting? O grave, where is thy victory?" (1 Corinthians 15:52-55). To those that accept Christ the promise is, "But he shall receive an hundredfold now in this time, houses, and brethren, and sisters, and mothers, and children, and lands, with persecutions; and in the world to come eternal life" (Mark 10:30).

1 John 5:16

If any man see his brother sin a sin which is not unto death, he shall ask, and he shall give him life for them that sin not unto death. There is a sin unto death: I do not say that he shall pray for it.

Answer

John is making a contrast between a person that sins a forgivable transgression (1 John 1:9), and one who commits the unpardonable sin. (See my notes on Matthew 12:31.) The rule of thumb is to pray and work for the salvation of those who may be yielding to practice sin. James writes, "Brethren, if any of you do err from the truth, and one convert him; Let him know, that he which converteth the sinner from the error of his way shall save a soul from death, and shall hide a multitude of sins" (James 5:19). Jude admonishes the believers to work for the salvation of erring brothers. "Keep yourselves in the love of God, looking for the mercy of our Lord Jesus Christ unto eternal life. And of some have compassion, making a difference: And others save with fear, pulling them out of the fire; hating even the garment spotted by the flesh" (Jude 21-23). God can answer intercessory prayer on the part of the faithful for those who are wavering, but if it is obvious that an individual has turned his or her back on God then there's not much that can be done for them.

Revelation 1:5

And from Jesus Christ, who is the faithful witness, and the first begotten of the dead, and the prince of the kings of the earth. Unto him that loved us, and washed us from our sins in his own blood.

Answer

In the Old Testament there were several people resurrected — the Shunammite boy (2 Kings 4:18-36) and others. The Lord resurrected several persons prior to His death: Lazarus (John 11) and the little damsel (Mark 5:40-42) among them. Jesus could not have been the "first begotten of the dead" in that sense. The word "first" connotes a sense of pre-eminence. Jacob was called the firstborn, but he was not. (See Genesis 25:34-36 and Exodus 4:22). King David is also called the firstborn (Psalm 89:19-27), but he is the youngest of seven sons (1 Chronicles 2:13-15). Notice in Psalm 89:27 that God said, "I will make him my firstborn, higher than the kings of the earth." All resurrections hinged on His. He was the only One who could claim, "Destroy this temple, and in three days I will raise it up" (John 2:19). "Therefore doth my Father love me, because I lay down my life, that I might take it again" (John 10:17). All those resurrected before died again. However, since He conquered death by His resurrection, His is preeminent!

Revelation 3:14

And unto the angel of the church of the Laodiceans write; These things saith the Amen, the faithful and true witness, the beginning of the creation of God.

Answer

This verse seems to imply that Christ is the beginning of creation. What it means is that He began creation. In Revelation Christ is referred to as the "Beginning." (See Revelation 1:8; 21:6; 22:13.) The Greek word *arche* used in chapter 3 is the same used in these other verses. In John chapter 1 we are told, "In the beginning was the Word, and the Word was with God, and the Word was God. The same was in the beginning with God. All things were made by him; and without him was not any thing made that was made" (John 1:1-3). It was the Word that became flesh (verse 14). In the book of Hebrews we find this verse: "Hath in these last days spoken unto us by his Son, whom he hath appointed heir of all things, by whom also he made the worlds" (Hebrews 1:2). Notice that Christ, the "Word," is said to have been in the beginning, and that He began all things, which He created.

Revelation 6:9-11

And when he had opened the fifth seal, I saw under the altar the souls of them that were slain for the word of God, and for the testimony which they held: And they cried with a loud voice, saying, How long, O Lord, holy and true, dost thou not judge and avenge our blood on them that dwell on the earth? And white robes were given unto every one of them; and it was said unto them, that they should rest yet for a little season, until their fellowservants also and their brethren, that should be killed as they were, should be fulfilled.

Answer

These "souls" are mentioned as not being in heaven, but "under the altar." There is no place in the Bible other than this text that uses such a phrase. This symbolism is referring to martyrs who gave their lives in sacrifice for the word of God. They are pictured as being below the altar (the altar representing the church that shed their blood), calling for justice. Jesus, referring to the same type of scenario, said, "From the blood of Abel unto the blood of Zacharias, which perished between the altar and the temple: verily I say unto you, It shall be required of this generation" (Luke 11:51). This personification is used in Genesis when God said to Cain, "What hast thou done? the voice of thy brother crieth out to me from the ground" (Genesis 4:10). These souls are told to "rest" until others should be killed (verse 11). This rest applies to those who are dead. It should be said here that these couldn't be in hell. They are said to be witnesses for the Word of God, and white robes are given them. Obviously, this is language that applies to those who are saved and not those who are lost. John writes concerning them, "Blessed are the dead which die in the Lord from henceforth: Yea, saith the Spirit, that they may rest from their labours; and their works do follow them" (Revelation 14:13). The dead are asleep; therefore, they are said to be resting. The plea for justice is finally answered when the seven last plagues are poured out. "And I heard the angel of the waters say, Thou art righteous, O Lord, which art, and wast, and shalt be, because thou hast judged thus. For they have shed the blood of saints and prophets, and thou hast given them blood to drink; for they are worthy. And I heard another out of the altar say, Even so, Lord God Almighty, true and righteous are thy judgments" (Revelation 16:5-7).

Revelation 14:10, 11

The same shall drink of the wine of the wrath of God, which is poured out without mixture into the cup of his indignation; and he shall be tormented with fire and brimstone in the presence of the holy angels, and in the presence of the Lamb: And the smoke of their torment ascendeth up for ever and ever: and they have no rest day nor night, who worship the beast and his image, and whosoever receiveth the mark of his name.

Answer

These verses, while employed to suggest that people who

have died are suffering eternal torment, are not dealing with the dead at all. These verses are revealing what shall happen to living people in the future that accept the mark of the beast. Notice it says, "Shall" [future] drink of the wrath of God." The question is when will this take place? The wrath of God is the "seven last plagues" (Revelation 15:1, 7; 16:1). It is during the outpouring of these plagues that men are scorched with fire. "And the fourth angel poured out his vial upon the sun; and power was given unto him to scorch men with fire. And men were scorched with great heat, and blasphemed the name of God, which hath power over these plagues: and they repented not to give him glory" (Revelation 16:8, 9). Though "scorched," and they "gnawed their tongues for pain" (verse 10), they continue in their rebellion. In chapter 18 it also includes the city called "Mystery Babylon the Great, the Mother of Harlots, and Abominations of the Earth" (Revelation 17:5). "Reward her even as she rewarded you, and double unto her double according to her works: in the cup which she hath filled fill to her double. How much she hath glorified herself, and lived deliciously, so much torment and sorrow give her: for she saith in her heart, I sit a queen, and am no widow, and shall see no sorrow. Therefore shall her plagues come in one day, death, and mourning, and famine; and she shall be utterly burned with fire: for strong is the Lord God who judgeth her" (Revelation 18:6-8). It is those responsible ("the seat of the Beast and his kingdom") for leading the world astray in apostasy against God that are the object of the burning. The city and its leaders are tormented with fire and then consumed, and it is the smoke of their torment, not their punishment, that ascends for ever. (See Revelation 18:9-19).

Revelation 20:10

And the devil that deceived them was cast into the lake of fire

and brimstone, where the beast and the false prophet are, and
shall be tormented day and night for ever and ever.

Answer

The term "forever" has several meanings, depending on the subject matter and the context. It can be used in several ways, for example: "She would love him forever," or used hyperbolically, "It took forever to get a passport." It can be used in slogans of support after the name of something or someone: "The Beatles Forever!" It can also have the sense of continually happening: "He was forever rubbing his nose." Jonah said that he was in the belly of the whale forever. He said, "I went down to the bottoms of the mountains; the earth with her bars was about me for ever: yet hast thou brought up my life from corruption, O LORD my God" (Jonah 2:6). Yet this "forever" was only three days and three nights (Jonah 1:17). The same usage of the word is found in reference to Samuel. He was to "remain in the temple forever" (1 Samuel 1:22), which meant as "long as he lives" (1 Samuel 1:28).

The revelator is describing the fact that whoever goes into the lake of fire will burn as long as the burning material is consumed forever. Notice that verse 9 says "fire came down from God out of heaven, and devoured them." This destruction is called the "second death" (Revelation 20:14; 21:8). Even the devil will be destroyed. "Thou hast defiled thy sanctuaries by the multitude of thine iniquities, by the iniquity of thy traffick; therefore will I bring forth a fire from the midst of thee, it shall devour thee, and I will bring thee to ashes upon the earth in the sight of all them that behold thee. All they that know thee among the people shall be astonished at thee: thou shalt be a terror, and never shalt thou be any more" (Ezekiel 28:18,19). And concerning those that follow him, Malachi wrote, "For, behold, the day cometh, that shall burn as an oven; and all the proud, yea, and all that do wickedly, shall be stubble: and the day that cometh shall burn them up, saith the LORD of hosts, that it shall leave them neither root nor branch. And ye shall tread down the wicked; for they shall be ashes under the soles of your feet in the day that I shall do this, saith the LORD of hosts" (Malachi 4:1, 3). Both the devil and the wicked will be turned into ashes. Yes, the wicked will burn day and night, or as long as it takes to destroy them forever.

Revelation 22:15

For without are dogs, and sorcerers, and whoremongers, and murderers, and idolaters, and whosoever loveth and maketh a lie.

Answer

This text has troubled pet owners who think that their dogs will not be permitted inside the kingdom. That there will be animals in the kingdom of God is clear from the writings of Isaiah. He writes, "The wolf also shall dwell with the lamb, and the leopard shall lie down with the kid; and the calf and the young lion and the fatling together; and a little child shall lead them. And the cow and the bear shall feed; their young ones shall lie down together: and the lion shall eat straw like the ox." "The wolf and the lamb shall feed together, and the lion shall eat straw like the bullock" (Isaiah 11: 6, 7; 65:25). The text in Revelation is not speaking about animals. It is addressing people who act or are involved in practices that are unacceptable to God. The word "dog" is used as an adjective describing a certain kind of person, just as the other words suggest that they are people who are sorcerers, whoremongers, murderers, idolaters, and liars. Notice how the word "dog" is used in the book of Isaiah. "His watchmen are blind: they are all ignorant, they are all dumb dogs, they cannot bark; sleeping, lying down, loving to slumber. Yea, they are greedy dogs which can never have enough, and they are shepherds that cannot understand: they all look to their own way, every one for his gain, from his quarter. Come ye, say they, I will fetch wine, and we will fill ourselves with strong drink; and to morrow shall be as this day, and much more abundant." Isaiah 56:10-12. Revelation is including in the list of vile sinners those ministers who are avaricious, self-centered, and are unfaithful to their sacred office.

Mission College of Evangelism not only trains laypersons and pastors for the work of ministry, but also has resources to help laypersons and pastors in their work of ministry.

Mission College of Evangelism
P.O. Box 769
38950 SW Laurelwood Rd.
Gaston, Oregon 97119
Web: www.mission-college.org
800-996-6477